# **200** healthy curries

# hamlyn | all colour cookbook

# 200 healthy curries

Sunil Vijayakar

An Hachette UK Company
www.hachette.co.uk

First published in Great Britain in 2012 by Hamlyn
a division of Octopus Publishing Group Ltd
Endeavour House, 189 Shaftesbury Avenue
London WC2H 8JY
www.octopusbooks.co.uk

ISBN: 978-0-600-62528-5

A CIP catalogue record for this book is available from the
British Library

Printed and bound in China

10 9 8 7 6 5 4 3 2 1

People with known nut allergies should avoid recipes
containing nuts or nut derivatives, and vulnerable people
should avoid dishes containing raw or lightly cooked eggs.

Both metric and imperial measurements have
been given in all recipes. Use one set of measurements
only, and not a mixture of both.

Standard level spoon measurements are used in all recipes
1 tablespoon = 15 ml spoon
1 teaspoon = 5 ml spoon

Ovens should be preheated to the specified temperature
– if using a fan-assisted oven, follow the manufacturer's
instructions for adjusting the time and temperature.

Fresh herbs should be used unless otherwise stated.

Medium eggs should be used unless otherwise stated.

Some of the recipes in this book have previously appeared
in other titles published by Hamlyn

# contents

# introduction

# introduction

Originating from the South Indian Tamil word *kari*, which means gravy or sauce, the word 'curry' literally refers to the spice blend used to flavour a dish. The word has evolved to describe a wide variety of saucy, spiced dishes from all over India, Southeast Asia, and even as far as Japan. We once used the word to describe an entire cuisine, but recently we have begun to discover the true diversity of our favourite food, and we are being introduced to authentic recipes from the many countries which provide spicy dishes that fall under the 'curry' umbrella.

A common perception is that a curry is a hot and spicy dish. Yes, you can eat a curry that will blow your socks off but, on the whole, most curry recipes are delicate and highly sophisticated, containing a balanced blend of spices and herbs.

As food lovers today, we have embraced curries from all over the world and count them among our favourite foods. There is nothing more satisfying to me than producing a rich, aromatic curry to share with friends and family. All you need are a storecupboard of spices and ingredients, some simple equipment and to learn some basic techniques.

## healthy favourites

Unfortunately, many curries contain a lot of oil, butter and cream, which are blended with herbs and spices to give rich but unhealthy dishes. The delicious recipes in this book will show you that you can cook healthy curries without compromising on flavour and taste. We have re-created your favourite curries – and some more unusual ones – without relying on unhealthy ingredients. We use them in much smaller quantities than usual and replace them with healthier options, like groundnut oil, which is much lower in saturated fat than ghee, sunflower oil or butter. We have used fat-free natural yogurt and reduced-fat coconut milk instead of cream and butter.

We have also omitted or reduced sugar and replaced it with agave syrup. Sweeter than honey, this organic, fat-free sweetener can replace sugar in many recipes – you only need a very small amount. Likewise, when seasoning your dishes, be sure to use salt sparingly as a high intake can contribute to high blood pressure and heart disease.

## basic ingredients

You can buy most of the ingredients you need for the recipes in this book in any large supermarket. Markets and ethnic food shops are great places to find the more unusual items, and they will stock large packets of spices at good prices. You can also order 'exotic' ingredients from specialist websites and have them delivered to your door.

## dry spices

The flavour of dry spices decreases with time, so buy them in small quantities and use them up quickly for best results.

### amchoor

Dried mango powder, used as a souring agent in Indian curries. Substitute with a little lemon juice or tamarind paste if unavailable.

### asafoetida

Also known as devil's dung, this plant resin can be bought in a lump or dried and ground in powder form. It is very strong in flavour. Usually used in tiny amounts in lentil dishes, it is believed to counteract flatulence.

### cardamom

This is usually used whole, in its pod, as an aromatic to flavour rice and curries. You can also use the little black seeds inside the pods on their own, by crushing them and using as part of a spice mixture or for a garam masala.

### cassia

Also known as Chinese cinnamon, cassia is an aromatic tree bark, which can be bought as sticks, rolled bark or powder form. It has a coarser texture and stronger flavour than cinnamon does.

### chilli

Whole dried red chillies add the fiery heat to a curry. Dried chilli flakes tend to have a milder flavour and chilli powders made from ground dried chillies vary in heat, ranging from mild or medium to hot.

### cinnamon

This sweet and warming aromatic spice comes from the bark of a tree and is available as sticks or rolled bark. Also widely used in ground powder form.

### cloves

These aromatic dried buds from an evergreen tree can be used whole or ground to a powder.

### coriander

The small, pale brown seeds of the coriander plant have a fresh, citrus flavour. Available whole or ground, they form the base of many curry pastes and dry spice mixes.

### cumin

Essential in Asian cooking, these small elongated brown seeds are used whole or ground, and have a distinctive, warm, pungent aroma. Whole seeds may be dry-roasted and sprinkled over a dish just before serving.

### curry powders

Ready-made curry powders are widely available and there are many different varieties, depending on the spice mix. Some are simply labelled mild, medium or hot, but there are many specific mixes, such as Tandoori Spice Mix or Madras Curry Powder.

### fennel seeds

These small, pale green seeds have a subtle aniseed flavour and are used as a flavouring in some spice mixes.

### fenugreek seeds

Usually square in shape, these tiny, shiny yellow seeds are used widely in pickles and ground into spice mixes for curries.

### garam masala

This common spice mix is usually added to a dish at the end of cooking time. A classic garam masala mix comprises cardamom, cloves, cumin, peppercorns, cinnamon and nutmeg. See page 78 for recipe.

### mustard seeds

Black, brown or yellow, these tiny round seeds are widely used as a flavouring to dishes and are usually fried in oil until they 'pop' to impart a mellow, nutty flavour.

### nigella seeds

Also known as black onion seeds or *kalonji*, these tiny, matt black, oval seeds are most frequently used to flavour breads and pickles.

### saffron

These deep orange strands are the dried stamens from a particular type of crocus and are used to give rice dishes and desserts a musky fragrance and golden colour.

### star anise

These dark brown, flower-shaped seed pods have a decidedly aniseed-like flavour.

### turmeric

This bright yellow-orange rhizome is widely available as a dried, ground powder. Turmeric has a warm, musky flavour and is used in small quantities to add flavour and colour to lentil and rice dishes and curries.

## fresh herbs & aromatics

It is essential to have a good selection of fresh herbs and aromatics to hand when making various different curries. Always buy the freshest ingredients you can find. Ethnic food shops are good places to buy aromatics such as such as Thai basil, lemon grass, kaffir lime leaves, coriander, mint and curry leaves, as they usually have a wide selection of fresh produce available at good prices. In case you have any left over, chillies, lemon grass, curry leaves and kaffir lime leaves all freeze very well for future use.

### chillies

Fresh green and red chillies are used in many types of curries to give heat and flavour. Much of the heat resides in the pith and seeds, so if you want to enjoy the chilli taste with less heat, make a long slit down the length of the chilli and carefully scrape out and discard the pith and seeds before slicing or chopping the flesh.

## coriander

The parsley of the East, fresh coriander is used widely in Asian cooking. Often the delicate leaves are used to flavour dishes, but the stalks and roots can also be used, especially in Thai curry pastes.

## curry leaves

These highly aromatic leaves are used fresh in Indian and Southeast Asian cooking. They come attached to stalks in sprays and are pulled off the stalks before use. Fresh curry leaves freeze very well and can be used straight from the freezer.

## galangal

This rhizome is used in the same way as its cousin ginger in savoury dishes. It is peeled and cut into very fine slivers or finely chopped. You can use fresh root ginger instead if you can't find any galangal.

## garlic

One of the essential flavours used in cooking all over the world, garlic cooked with ginger and onion forms the base of many curries. It is used sliced, crushed or grated.

## ginger

Another indispensable aromatic, fresh root ginger has a fresh, peppery flavour and is used in both savoury and sweet dishes.

## kaffir lime leaves

The leaves from the knobbly kaffir lime are highly aromatic. When used in a curry, they are usually finely shredded but are sometimes left whole. They freeze very well and can be used straight from the freezer.

## lemon grass

Known as *sere* in Indonesia, *serai* in Malaysia, *takrai* in Thailand and *tanglad* in the Phillipines, this green grass is used for its citrus flavour and aroma. It can be used whole by bruising the base of the stalk, or can be finely sliced or chopped. Remove the tough outer leaves before slicing or chopping as they can be very fibrous.

## onions

This humble vegetable forms the base of many curries. Sliced or chopped, it is usually slowly fried before the other ingredients are added. Store onions in a wire basket in the kitchen at room temperature.

### shallots

These small, sweet and pungent members of the onion family are widely used in Southeast Asian cooking. To peel them, slice them in half and only then remove the outer skin.

### Thai basil

Found in Oriental food shops, this delicate herb is used to garnish and flavour curries. You can substitute regular basil if you cannot find any.

## other useful ingredients

### coconut milk and coconut cream

Widely used in Asian cooking, canned coconut milk is readily available. It is added to curries to impart a rich, creamy texture. Coconut cream is a thicker, richer version. For a healthier option, use reduced-fat coconut milk.

### gram flour

Also known as *besan*, this pale yellow flour, made from dried chickpeas, is used widely for thickening and binding, as well as being the main ingredient in savoury batters.

### palm sugar

Known as *jaggery* in India and *nam tan peep* in Thailand, this is the sugar produced from the sap of various kinds of palms. Sold in cakes or cans, palm sugar has a deep, caramel flavour and is light brown in colour. It is used in curries to balance the spices. You can use any brown sugar as a substitute.

### shrimp paste

Also known as *kapee*, this is a pungent preserve used in Asian cooking. Made by pounding shrimp with salt and leaving it to decompose, it has a powerful aroma, which disappears when cooked.

### sweet chilli sauce

This sweet and mild sauce is made from red chillies, sugar, garlic and vinegar.

### tamarind paste

Used as a souring agent in curries, the paste from the tamarind pod can be used straight from the jar. You can also buy it in semi-dried pulp form, which needs to be soaked in warm water and strained before use.

### Thai fish sauce

Also known as *nam pla*, this sauce is made from the liquid extracted from salted, fermented fish and is one of the main ingredients in Thai cooking.

# cooking perfect rice

Rice is the basic accompaniment to curries served all over the world and makes a perfect foil to the spices. There are many different techniques for cooking rice. One of the simplest is the absorption method, where the rice is cooked in in a covered pan with a measured amount of liquid until all the liquid has been absorbed. As the liquid is absorbed, steam finishes the cooking, and the rice is tender and fluffy. For alternative ways of cooking rice, see pages 104 and 156.

Cooking perfect rice is easy if you follow these simple steps. For best results, measure rice by volume, not weight.

### step one

Rinse the rice in a few changes of cold running water. The rinsing removes any loose starch, and will make the rice less sticky.

Usually, you can get good results without soaking your rice. If using older rice, however, soak it in cold water for 15–30 minutes, as this makes the grains less brittle and prone to breakage. Soaking is also traditional for basmati rice, as it helps the rice expand to its maximum length during cooking.

Whether you soak it or not, be sure to drain your rice thoroughly after rinsing or you'll be using more water during cooking than you intended.

### step two

As stated above, the absorption method is the simplest way to cook rice. The key to this method is figuring out the correct amount of water or stock. The general rule is to use 1½ to 1¾ cups of water (or stock) to each cup of basmati or long-grain white rice, but you may need to experiment a little to find the amount you like best. Brown rice requires more water, while short-grain rice requires less. Keep in mind that more water gives you softer, stickier rice and less water results in firmer rice.

A heat diffuser is an important piece of equipment to use when cooking rice, as it will distribute the heat evenly under the saucepan and prevent burning. The other important element is a heavy-based saucepan to prevent scorching on the bottom, with a tight-fitting lid to keep the steam in. If your lid fits loosely, put a piece of foil or a clean kitchen cloth between the lid and the pot.

### step three

Place the rice in the saucepan with the measured amount of liquid and bring it to the boil. Cover tightly and reduce the heat to low. After 12–15 minutes, the liquid should have been absorbed, and the rice just tender.

If you served the rice now, you'd find the top layer dry and fluffy, and the bottom moist and fragile. Here's where you need patience: remove the pan from the heat and let the rice sit undisturbed with the lid on, for at least 5 minutes and for as long as 30. This lets the moisture redistribute, resulting in a more uniform texture, with the bottom layer as fluffy as the top.

## stir-frying rice

For perfect fried rice, with loose separate grains, it is important to use cold cooked rice and to heat the frying pan or wok until it is really hot before you add the rice. When a recipe calls for cold cooked rice, you should use rice that has been cooled quickly after it has been cooked and then stored in the refrigerator until ready to use in your recipe.

## essential equipment

You will not need any expensive or complicated equipment to cook curries, but a few essential items will help you prepare them in an easy and efficient manner. You will need the basic tools that every kitchen usually has – such as ladles, spoons, sieves, colanders, chopping boards and knives – but a few other items are well worthwhile having.

### grinding & blending

The secret of any good curry is the base, a mixture of a number of spices and herbs combined to form a dry curry powder or a wet curry paste. A mortar and pestle is the traditional method of combining the ingredients and is always reliable, but it does involve quite a lot of elbow grease.

Alternatively, you can use an electric coffee grinder for grinding dry spices. They are inexpensive and widely available, but make sure you keep one grinder just for spices, or your coffee will end up tasting fairly strange.

When you have to grind or blend together wet ingredients and dry spices to make a curry paste, a mini blender is invaluable, as it will give you a smooth mixture with ease. Most standard food processors are simply too big to handle small quantities effectively.

### stove-top cooking

Choose heavy-based saucepans, frying pans and woks. The thick base will ensure the food is heated evenly, without burning or sticking to the base of the pan, especially when it is cooked for a long, slow period. A large pan with a tight-fitting lid will be invaluable.

Even with a heavy-based pan, a heat diffuser is very useful for gentle cooking. This is a disc made from perforated metal, usually with a removable handle, that sits on top of the heat source. You place your pan on top and it is especially useful when an even, low, well-distributed heat is required, for example for slow-cooking curries and for perfectly

cooked rice. Inexpensive heat diffusers are widely available from good kitchen shops and they will last you for years.

## curry powders & pastes

Most curry recipes call for a curry powder or paste. Many of the recipes in this book give instructions for making one, while others use a standard curry powder or a common paste such as Thai green curry paste.

While ready-made powders and pastes are easily available, and many are very good, making your own will turn a good curry into something quite sublime. Make a big batch when you have the time, and store dry powders in airtight jars in the refrigerator and fresh pastes in the freezer to make several lovely curries in the weeks to come.

### basic curry powder
Makes about 125 g (4 oz)

2 tablespoons **ground coriander**
2 teaspoons **ground turmeric**
½ teaspoon **black mustard seeds**
¼ teaspoon **fenugreek seeds**
6–8 dried **curry leaves**
2 tablespoons **cumin seeds**
1 teaspoon **black peppercorns**
1–6 dried **red chillies**, roughly broken
1 teaspoon **cardamom seeds**
1 **cinnamon** or **cassia bark stick**
5–6 **cloves**
¼ teaspoon **ground ginger**

For a mild curry powder, use 1–2 dried red chillies; for a medium curry powder, use 3–4; and for a hot curry powder use 5–6 chillies. Dry-roast all the ingredients in a nonstick frying pan over a low heat for 2–3 minutes until fragrant. Remove from the heat and allow to cool. Tip the contents of the pan into a mini blender or clean electric coffee grinder, and grind to a fine powder. Store in an airtight container for up to 1 month, or in the refrigerator for up to 3 months.

## thai green curry paste
Makes 150–180 ml (5–6 fl oz)

2 teaspoons **ground coriander**
2 teaspoons **ground cumin**
1 teaspoon **white peppercorns**
4–6 fresh **long green chillies**, chopped
4 **shallots**, finely chopped
2 tablespoons chopped **garlic**
2 teaspoons finely chopped **kaffir lime leaves**
2 tablespoons chopped **lemon grass** (tough outer leaves removed)
1 tablespoon peeled and finely chopped **galangal** or **fresh root ginger**
2 teaspoons **shrimp paste**
1 tablespoon **groundnut oil**

Grind all the ingredients to a smooth paste with a mortar and pestle or mini blender. Store in an airtight container in the refrigerator for up to 1 month, or freeze in small portions to use as needed.

## thai red curry paste
Makes 150 ml (5 fl oz)

2 teaspoons **ground coriander**
1 teaspoon **ground cumin**
1 teaspoon **white peppercorns**
8 dried long **red chillies**, deseeded and finely chopped
2 tablespoons finely grated **garlic**
2 tablespoons finely chopped **lemon grass** (tough outer leaves removed)
1 tablespoon peeled and finely chopped **galangal or fresh root ginger**
3 fresh **coriander roots**, finely chopped
2 teaspoons finely chopped **kaffir lime leaves**
2 teaspoons **shrimp paste**
2 tablespoons **groundnut oil**

Grind all the ingredients to a smooth paste with a mortar and pestle or mini blender. Store in an airtight container in the refrigerator for up to 1 month, or freeze in small portions to use as needed.

# starters & snacks

# spicy potato & apple salad

Serves **4**

Preparation time **20 minutes**, plus chilling

1 tablespoon freshly crushed **black pepper**

1 tablespoon **cumin seeds**, dry-roasted and roughly ground

3 teaspoons **amchoor**

1 teaspoon **chilli powder**

2 **red apples**

3 **waxy potatoes**, peeled, boiled and diced

1 small **cucumber**, diced

juice of 2 **limes**

handful of chopped **coriander** and **mint**

**salt** and **pepper**

**Mix** together the four spices and set aside.

**Core** the apples, and cut the flesh into small cubes. Put in a bowl with the potatoes, cucumber and lime juice, sprinkle over the spice mixture, season and toss to mix well.

**Cover** the bowl and marinate in the refrigerator for 30 minutes to allow the flavours to develop. Just before serving, toss in the herbs. Mix well and serve immediately.

### For potato & apple salad with spiced creamy dressing, place 1 diced green chilli, 2 crushed garlic cloves, the juice of 2 limes, 1 teaspoon agave syrup, 1 tablespoon mild curry powder, ¼ teaspoon turmeric and 300 ml (½ pint) fat-free natural yogurt in a food processor and blend until smooth. Place 3 peeled, boiled and diced potatoes in a salad bowl with 2 diced apples, ½ sliced red onion and ½ sliced cucumber. Drizzle over the dressing, toss to mix well and serve.

# green masala chicken kebabs

Serves **4**
Preparation time **10 minutes**,
   plus marinating
Cooking time **10 minutes**

4 skinless **chicken breast
   fillets**, cubed
juice of 1 **lime**
100 ml (3½ fl oz) **fat-free
   natural yogurt**
1 teaspoon peeled and finely
   grated **fresh root ginger**
1 **garlic clove**, crushed
1 **fresh green chilli**, deseeded
   and chopped
large handful of finely chopped
   **coriander leaves**
large handful of finely chopped
   **mint leaves**
1 tablespoon **medium curry
   powder** (see page 18)
pinch of **salt**
**lime wedges**, to serve

**Place** the chicken in a large bowl. Place all the
remaining ingredients in a food processor and blend
until smooth, adding a little water if necessary. Pour over
the chicken, and toss to mix well. Cover and leave to
marinate in the refrigerator overnight.

**Preheat** the grill until hot. Thread the chicken on to
8 metal skewers, and grill for 6–8 minutes, turning once
or twice, until the chicken is cooked through. Serve
immediately with lime wedges for squeezing.

**For red masala chicken kebabs**, mix 4 tablespoons
fat-free natural yogurt with 4 tablespoons tomato purée,
1 teaspoon grated ginger, 4 crushed garlic cloves,
1 tablespoon chilli powder, 1 teaspoon ground cumin
and 1 teaspoon turmeric. Pour over the chicken and
marinate and cook as above.

# coconut, carrot & spinach salad

Serves **4**
Preparation time **10 minutes**
Cooking time **1 minute**

300 g (10 oz) **baby spinach**,
  finely chopped
1 **carrot**, coarsely grated
25 g (1 oz) **fresh coconut**,
  grated
2 tablespoons **groundnut oil**
2 teaspoons **black mustard
  seeds**
1 teaspoon **cumin seeds**
juice of **1 lime**
juice of **1 orange**
**salt** and **pepper**

**Place** the spinach in a large bowl with the carrot and coconut, and toss together lightly.

**Heat** the oil a small frying pan over a medium heat. Add the mustard and cumin seeds, and stir-fry for 20–30 seconds until fragrant and the mustard seeds start to 'pop'.

**Remove** from the heat, and pour over the salad with the lime and orange juice. Season well and toss before serving.

**For spicy coconut, carrot & spinach sauté**, heat 1 tablespoon groundnut oil in a large wok or frying pan and add 1 finely diced red chilli, 2 finely chopped garlic cloves, 4 finely sliced spring onions and 1 teaspoon each of cumin and black mustard seeds. Stir-fry for 1 minute, then add 1 coarsely grated carrot. Stir-fry for 2–3 minutes and add 200 g (7 oz) baby spinach. Stir-fry over a high heat for 2–3 minutes or until the spinach has just wilted. Season, sprinkle with 25 g (1 oz) grated fresh coconut and serve immediately.

# chilled tomato & yogurt soup

Serves **4**
Preparation time **5 minutes**,
plus chilling

750 g (1½ lb) **tomatoes**,
peeled, deseeded and
chopped
2 tablespoons **lemon juice**
1 tablespoon **white wine
vinegar**
1 teaspoon **mild curry
powder** (see page 18)
250 ml (8 fl oz) **fat-free
natural yogurt**, whisked
**salt** and **pepper**
small handful of chopped
**coriander leaves**, to garnish

**Place** the tomatoes, lemon juice, vinegar, curry powder
and yogurt in a food processor and blend until smooth.
Season well, transfer to a bowl, cover and chill in the
refrigerator for 3–4 hours or overnight.

**Ladle** the soup into chilled soup bowls, garnish with a
sprinkling of chopped coriander and serve immediately.

**For chilled spicy cucumber & yogurt soup**, replace
the tomatoes with 2 large peeled, deseeded and diced
cucumbers and 4 finely sliced spring onions. Blend and
chill as above. To serve, sprinkle with 1 tablespoon dry-
roasted cumin seeds and a small handful of chopped
mint leaves.

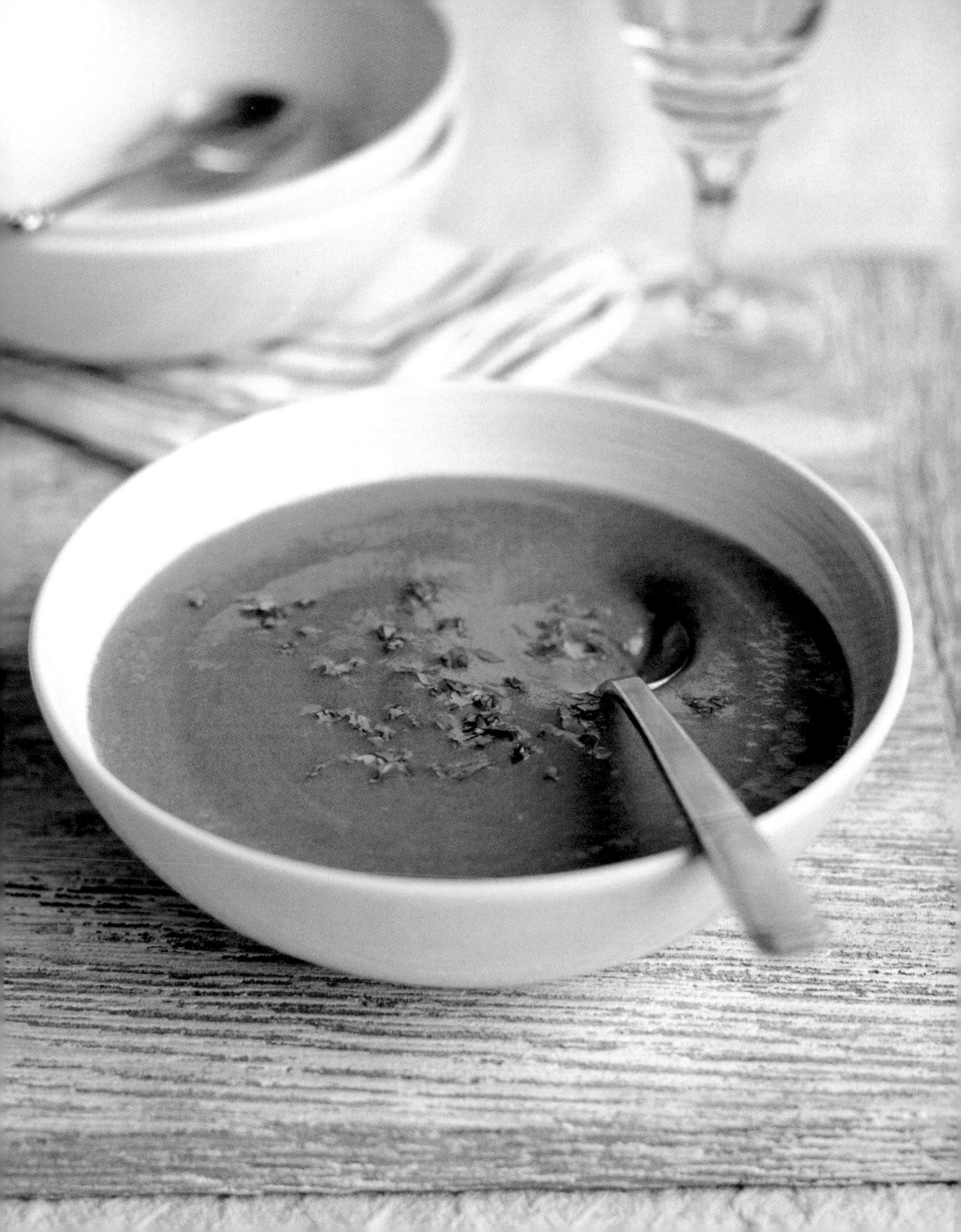

# chilli & king prawn salad

Serves **4**
Preparation time **10 minutes**
Cooking time **3–4 minutes**

1 teaspoon **sesame oil**
250 g (8 oz) **raw king prawns**,
  peeled and deveined
4 **spring onions**, thinly sliced
  on the diagonal
10 cm (4 in) piece of
  **cucumber**, deseeded and
  cut into matchsticks
16 **cherry tomatoes**, halved
1 tablespoon finely chopped
  **coriander leaves**
1 teaspoon **Thai fish sauce**
2 **fresh red chillies**, finely
  chopped
4 tablespoons **lemon juice**

**Heat** the oil in a large wok or frying pan over a medium-high heat. When the oil is hot, add the prawns and stir-fry for 3–4 minutes until they turn pink.

**Remove** the prawns from the pan with a slotted spoon, and cut into thin slices on the diagonal. Place them in a bowl with the remaining ingredients and toss to mix well. Serve immediately.

**For spicy chicken & chilli salad**, mix 5 tablespoons lemon juice with 4 tablespoons sweet chilli sauce, 2 tablespoons light soy sauce, 1 finely diced red chilli and 1 teaspoon sesame oil. Place 3 shredded cooked chicken breasts in a wide bowl and add 6 thinly sliced spring onions, 16 halved cherry tomatoes, ½ sliced cucumber and a large handful of coriander leaves. Spoon over the dressing, toss to mix well and serve.

# pork, potato & pea samosas

Makes **20**
Preparation time **20 minutes**,
  plus chilling
Cooking time **25 minutes**

1 tablespoon **groundnut oil**
300 g (10 oz) **minced pork**
1 **onion**, chopped
1 tablespoon **medium curry
  powder** (see page 16)
50 g (2 oz) **potato**, peeled,
  boiled and finely diced
50 g (2 oz) **frozen peas**
4 tablespoons chopped
  **coriander leaves**
4 tablespoons chopped **mint
  leaves**
5 **filo pastry sheets**, each
  25 x 50 cm (10 x 20 inches)
1 **egg**, beaten
**cooking oil spray**
**salt** and **pepper**

**Heat** the oil in a frying pan over a medium heat. Add
the pork, onion and curry powder, season and cook for
about 10 minutes until the pork is just cooked and the
juices have evaporated from the pan. Add the potatoes
and peas and mix well. Remove the pan from the heat,
add the chopped herbs and set aside to cool.

**Lay** the filo pastry sheets in a stack on a clean board.
Cut into quarters to give 4 rectangles from each sheet.
Cover the pastry with a barely damp tea towel to
prevent it drying out.

**Lay** one sheet of filo on the work surface with a short
side nearest you. Place a dessertspoonful of the filling
on the end nearest you and fold the bottom right
corner of the pastry over to meet the left hand side and
enclose the filling in a triangle. Continue folding the
parcel over down the length of the pastry to make a
neat triangular parcel. Brush the loose edge with a little
of the beaten egg to seal, then place on a baking sheet.
Repeat to make 20 samosas, then brush them with
beaten egg and chill until ready to cook.

**Preheat** the oven to 220°C (425°F), Gas Mark 7. Lightly
spray the samosas with cooking oil spray and cook for
12–15 minutes oven until golden brown. Serve warm.

**For mint & yogurt chutney**, to serve as an
accompaniment, place a large handful of chopped mint
leaves in a blender with a small handful of chopped
coriander leaves, 1 finely chopped green chilli, 2 chopped
garlic cloves, 1 teaspoon grated root ginger, the juice of
2 limes, 2 teaspoons agave syrup and 300 ml (½ pint)
fat-free natural yogurt. Season and blend until smooth.

# mint, spinach & buttermilk shorba

Serves **4**
Preparation time **10 minutes**

250 g (8 oz) **frozen spinach**,
    defrosted
1 **garlic clove**, crushed
1 teaspoon **mild curry
    powder** (see page 16)
½ teaspoon peeled and finely
    grated **fresh root ginger**
500 ml (17 fl oz) **buttermilk**
6 tablespoons finely chopped
    **mint leaves**, plus extra to
    garnish
350 ml (12 fl oz) **iced water**
8 **ice cubes**
**salt** and **pepper**

**Place** the spinach in a colander and squeeze out the excess water. Chop the spinach very finely.

**Transfer** to a food processor with the garlic, curry powder, ginger and buttermilk. Season well and stir in the chopped mint. Add the measured water and process the mixture until smooth.

**Ladle** the soup into chilled bowls, drop 2 ice cubes into each bowl and garnish with a few extra mint leaves. Serve immediately.

**For curried spinach & potato soup**, place 300 g (10 oz) finely chopped spinach in a saucepan with 1 finely chopped onion, 2 crushed garlic cloves, 1 teaspoon finely grated ginger, 1 finely chopped red chilli, 1 teaspoon mild curry powder (see page 16) and 900 ml (1½ pints) vegetable stock. Bring to the boil. Peel 2 medium potatoes, cut into 1.5 cm (¾ inch) dice and add to the spinach mixture. Bring back to the boil, reduce the heat and simmer for 15–20 minutes or until the potato is tender. Season and serve in warmed bowls.

# peanut & cucumber salad

Serves **4**
Preparation time **5 minutes**
Cooking time **5 minutes**

1 large **cucumber**, peeled and
   finely chopped
4 tablespoons **lemon juice**
1 tablespoon **light olive oil**
1 teaspoon **yellow mustard
   seeds**
2 teaspoons **black mustard
   seeds**
8–10 **curry leaves**
1–2 **fresh red chillies**,
   deseeded and finely
   chopped
4 tablespoons finely chopped
   **roasted peanuts**
**salt** and **pepper**

**Place** the cucumber in a large bowl, sprinkle over the lemon juice and season with salt. Stir to mix well and set aside.

**Heat** the oil in a small frying pan over a medium heat. Add the mustard seeds, curry leaves and chilli, and stir-fry for 1–2 minutes until fragrant and the mustard seeds start to 'pop'.

**Add** the contents of the pan to the cucumber mixture. Toss to mix well, sprinkle over the chopped peanuts and serve immediately.

**For spicy roasted tomato salad**, cut 10 midi plum tomatoes in half and place on a baking sheet, cut side up. Season and sprinkle over 1 tablespoon mild curry powder (see page 16) and 2 teaspoons cumin seeds. Lightly spray with cooking oil spray and roast in a preheated oven at 200°C (400°F), Gas Mark 6, for 12–15 minutes. Allow to cool. Arrange 200 g (7 oz) mixed salad leaves on a wide serving platter with ½ sliced red onion. Arrange the cooled tomatoes over the salad, squeeze over the juice of 2 limes and sprinkle with 4 tablespoons toasted pumpkin seeds.

# hara boti kebabs

Serves **4**

Preparation time **20 minutes**,
   plus marinating

Cooking time **12–15 minutes**

750 g (1½ lb) **lean leg of
   lamb**, cubed

1 **onion**, finely chopped

2 teaspoons **garlic salt**

2 teaspoons **ground ginger**

1 tablespoon **ground cumin**

1 tablespoon **mild curry
   powder** (see page 16)

1 tablespoon **mild chilli
   powder**

1 tablespoon **fennel seeds**

6 tablespoons finely chopped
   **coriander leaves**

2 tablespoons finely chopped
   **mint leaves**

250 ml (8 fl oz) **fat-free
   natural yogurt**

½ teaspoon **agave syrup**

juice of 2 **limes**

**salt** and **pepper**

**Place** the lamb in a large non-metallic dish. Place all the remaining ingredients in a food processor and blend until smooth. Season well and pour over the lamb. Cover and marinate in the refrigerator for 24–48 hours.

**Remove** the lamb from the refrigerator, and allow to come to room temperature. Preheat the oven to 200°C (400°F), Gas Mark 6.

**Thread** the lamb on to 8–12 metal skewers, and arrange on a baking sheet lined with greaseproof paper. Cook in the preheated oven for 12–15 minutes until tender and cooked through.

**For cumin, chilli & lemon rice**, to serve as an accompaniment, place 2 teaspoons cumin seeds in a saucepan with 1 diced red chilli, 1 teaspoon ground turmeric, the finely grated rind and juice of 1 lemon, 300 g (10 oz) basmati rice and 650 ml (1 pint 2 fl oz) hot vegetable stock. Season and bring to the boil. Reduce the heat to low, cover the pan and cook gently for 10–12 minutes or until all the liquid has been absorbed. Remove from the heat and allow to stand, covered and undisturbed, for 10–15 minutes. Fluff up the grains with a fork and serve.

# carrot & red cabbage slaw

Serves **4**
Preparation time **10 minutes**
Cooking time **1 minute**

3 large **carrots**, coarsely
  grated
300 g (10 oz) **red cabbage**,
  finely shredded
juice of 2 **limes**
2 teaspoons **agave syrup**
2 tablespoons **light olive oil**
1 fresh **red chilli**, finely diced
1 tablespoon **black mustard
  seeds**
**salt** and **pepper**

**Place** the carrots and red cabbage in a large bowl.
Mix together the lime juice and agave syrup, and stir
into the vegetables. Toss to mix well, and set aside.

**Heat** the oil in a small frying pan over a medium
heat. Add the chilli and mustard seeds, and stir-fry
for 20–30 seconds until fragrant and the mustard
seeds start to 'pop'.

**Scrape** the contents of the frying pan over the salad,
season well and toss to combine. Serve immediately.

**For toasted spiced chapati wedges**, to serve
as an accompaniment, cut 4 ready-made chapatis
into wedges and arrange on 2 large baking sheets.
Lightly spray with cooking oil spray and sprinkle over
1 tablespoon crushed cumin seeds, 1 tablespoon
nigella seeds, 2 teaspoons mild chilli powder and a little
sea salt. Cook in a preheated oven at 180°C (350°F),
Gas Mark 4, for 8–10 minutes or until crisp. Serve hot.

# chilli-seared squid & herb salad

Serves **4**
Preparation time **15 minutes**, plus marinating
Cooking time **10 minutes**

large pinch of **sea salt**
1 teaspoon **ground coriander**
1 teaspoon **ground cumin**
1 teaspoon **hot chilli powder**
8 tablespoons **lemon juice**
1 teaspoon **tomato purée**
1 **fresh red chilli**, deseeded and finely sliced
1 teaspoon peeled and finely grated **fresh root ginger**
1 **garlic clove**, crushed
750 g (1½ lb) **squid**, cut into bite-sized pieces
1 small **red onion**, very thinly sliced
large handful of chopped **coriander leaves**
small handful of chopped **mint leaves**

**Mix** the salt, ground spices, chilli powder, lemon juice, tomato purée, chilli, ginger and garlic in a large bowl and add the squid. Toss to coat evenly, cover and leave to stand at room temperature for 15 minutes.

**Heat** a nonstick ridged griddle pan over a very high heat. Working in batches, lift the squid from the marinade and sear in the hot pan for 1–2 minutes, then remove from the pan and keep warm while you cook the remaining squid.

**Add** the red onion and herbs to the cooked squid, toss to mix well and serve immediately.

**For king prawn, mango & herb salad**, replace the squid with 750 g (1½ lb) raw peeled king prawns. Marinate in the spice mixture for 10 minutes, then cook in the smoking hot pan in batches for 2–3 minutes on each side, or until pink and cooked through. Transfer to a wide salad bowl and stir in a large handful each of coriander and mint leaves and the diced flesh of 1 ripe mango. Toss to mix well and serve

# spicy courgette fritters

Serves **4**
Preparation time **15 minutes**,
  plus draining
Cooking time **10–15 minutes**

3 **courgettes**
2 large **spring onions**, grated
1 **garlic clove**, finely chopped
finely grated rind of **1 lemon**
4 tablespoons **gram flour**
2 teaspoons **medium curry
  powder** (see page 16)
1 **fresh red chilli**, deseeded
  and finely chopped
2 tablespoons finely chopped
  **mint leaves**
2 tablespoons finely chopped
  **coriander leaves**
2 **eggs**, lightly beaten
2 tablespoons **light olive oil**
**salt** and **pepper**

**Grate** the courgettes into a colander. Sprinkle lightly with salt and leave for at least 1 hour to drain. Squeeze out the remaining liquid.

**Place** the remaining ingredients, except the eggs and olive oil, in a mixing bowl and add the courgettes. Season lightly, bearing in mind you have already salted the courgettes, and mix well. Add the eggs and mix again to combine.

**Heat** half the olive oil in a large frying pan over a medium-high heat. Place dessertspoonfuls of the mixture, well spaced, in the pan and press down with the back of the spoon. Cook for 1–2 minutes on each side, until golden and cooked through. Remove from the pan and keep warm. Repeat to cook the rest of the fritters in the same way, adding the remaining oil to the pan when necessary.

**For cucumber, mango & fromage frais relish**, to serve as an accompaniment, peel, deseed and coarsely grate 1 cucumber into a fine mesh sieve. Squeeze out any excess liquid using the back of a spoon. Place the grated cucumber in a bowl with 2 tablespoons hot mango chutney and 200 g (7 oz) fat-free fromage frais. Stir in a small handful of finely chopped coriander leaves, season and chill until required.

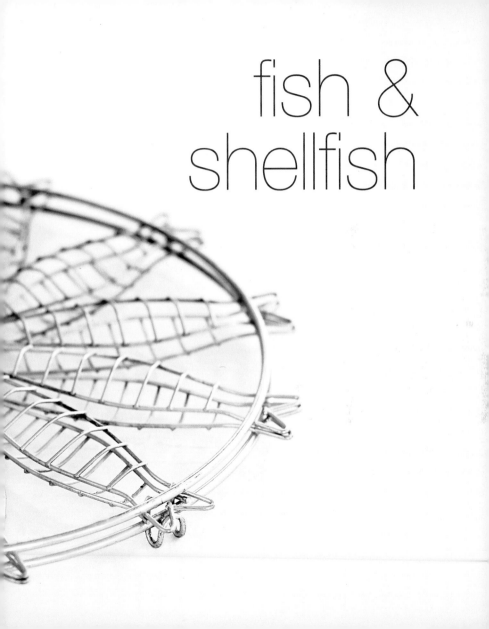

fish &
shellfish

# cambodian fish curry

Serves **4**
Preparation time **10 minutes**
Cooking time **15 minutes**

2 tablespoons finely chopped
   **lemon grass** (tough outer
   leaves removed)
1 tablespoon peeled and finely
   chopped **galangal**
3 **fresh red chillies**, roughly
   chopped
4 **garlic cloves**, roughly
   chopped
200 ml (7 fl oz) **water**
750 g (1½ lb) thick **halibut
   fillet**, skinned and cubed
1 tablespoon **groundnut oil**
200 ml (7 fl oz) **reduced-fat
   coconut milk**
1 tablespoon **Thai fish sauce**
2 tablespoons chopped **dry-
   roasted peanuts**
small handful of **Thai basil
   leaves**

**Place** the lemon grass, galangal, chillies and garlic in
a mini blender with the measured water and blend to a
smooth paste. Set aside.

**Pat** the fish dry with kitchen paper, arrange on a grill
rack and cook under a medium-hot grill for 10–12
minutes or until cooked through.

**Meanwhile,** heat the oil in a nonstick frying pan and
stir-fry the spice paste for 4–5 minutes. Add the
coconut milk and fish sauce and cook, stirring, over a
high heat for 5 minutes. Add the fish to the pan with
the peanuts and basil, and toss gently to mix well. Serve
immediately.

**For spicy fish with lemon grass & coconut**, place
4 thick cod fillets in a shallow, lightly greased ovenproof
dish in a single layer. Mix together 2 tablespoons
finely chopped lemon grass, 2 finely chopped fresh
red chillies, 2 teaspoons each of grated fresh root
ginger and garlic and 100 ml (3½ fl oz) reduced-fat
coconut milk. Season and spoon over the fish. Cook
in a preheated oven at 180°C (350°F), Gas Mark 4,
for 15–20 minutes or until cooked through. Serve
garnished with chopped coriander.

# dry prawn curry

Serves **4**

Preparation time **10 minutes**

Cooking time **10 minutes**

1 **onion**, roughly chopped

4 **garlic cloves**, chopped

8 tablespoons **lemon juice**

1 teaspoon peeled and finely
grated **fresh root ginger**

1 teaspoon **ground turmeric**

½ teaspoon **chilli powder**

2 teaspoons **shop-bought
medium curry paste**

1 tablespoon **groundnut oil**

500 g (1 lb) **raw tiger prawns**,
peeled and deveined

4 tablespoons chopped
**coriander leaves**

4 **spring onions**, finely sliced

**salt**

**Place** the onion, garlic, lemon juice, ginger, turmeric,
chilli powder and curry paste in a food processor and
blend until fairly smooth. Season with salt.

**Heat** the oil in a wide saucepan over a medium heat.
Add the onion paste and stir-fry for 2–3 minutes. Add
the prawns and stir-fry for a further 4–5 minutes until
they turn pink and are cooked through.

**Remove** from the heat and stir in the coriander and
spring onions. Serve immediately.

**For lemon & herbed couscous**, to serve as an
accompaniment, place 300 g (10 oz) couscous in
a shallow heatproof bowl. Add boiling water to just
cover the couscous, cover tightly and allow to stand for
12–15 minutes. Fluff up the grains of the couscous
with a fork, season and stir in a large handful each of
chopped coriander and mint. Squeeze over the juice of
1 lemon and serve immediately.

# thai mussel curry with ginger

Serves **4**
Preparation time **30 minutes**
Cooking time **15 minutes**

½–1 **fresh red chilli**
2 **shallots**, quartered
1 **lemon grass stalk**
1 tablespoon peeled and finely
   chopped **fresh root ginger**
1 tablespoon **groundnut oil**
400 ml (14 fl oz) **reduced-fat
   coconut milk**
4–5 **kaffir lime leaves**
150 ml (¼ pint) **fish stock**
2 teaspoons **Thai fish sauce**
1.5 kg (3 lb) **mussels**,
   scrubbed and debearded
small bunch of **coriander**, torn
   into pieces, to garnish

**Place** the chilli, shallots, lemon grass and ginger into a mini blender and blend until finely chopped.

**Heat** the oil in large, deep saucepan, add the finely chopped ingredients and fry over a medium heat for 5 minutes, stirring until softened. Add the coconut milk, lime leaves, fish stock and fish sauce and cook for 3 minutes.

**Add** the mussels, cover the pan and cook for about 5 minutes or until the mussel shells have opened, discarding any that do not open. Spoon into warmed bowls and serve garnished with coriander.

**For Thai chicken & aubergine curry**, prepare the above recipe up to the end of the second step, replacing the fish stock with 250 ml (8 fl oz) chicken stock. Stir in 1 diced aubergine and 300 g (10 oz) chicken breast, cut into large chunks. Bring back to the boil, cover and simmer for 12–15 minutes, or until the chicken is cooked and the aubergine tender. Serve scattered with coriander.

# cochin fish curry

Serves **4**
Preparation time **15 minutes**
Cooking time **30–35 minutes**

1 **onion**, chopped
4 **garlic cloves**, crushed
2 **fresh green chillies**,
   deseeded and chopped
1 tablespoon **ground cumin**
1 teaspoon **ground coriander**
1 teaspoon **ground turmeric**
small handful of finely chopped
   **coriander leaves**, plus extra
   to garnish
200 ml (7 fl oz) **water**
1 tablespoon **groundnut oil**
6 **curry leaves**
400 ml (14 fl oz) reduced-fat
   **coconut milk**
875 g (1¾ lb) thick **cod** or
   **halibut fillet**, skinned and
   cubed
**salt** and **pepper**

**Place** the onion, garlic, chillies, cumin, ground coriander, turmeric, coriander leaves and measured water in a food processor and blend to a smooth paste.

**Heat** the oil in a large frying pan over a high heat. Add the curry leaves and stir-fry for 20–30 seconds. Now add the blended paste and cook, stirring, over a high heat for 3–4 minutes until fragrant. Reduce the heat, pour in the coconut milk and simmer gently, uncovered, for 20 minutes.

**Add** the fish to the pan in a single layer and bring back to the boil. Reduce the heat and simmer gently for 5–6 minutes until the fish is just cooked through. Season and remove from the heat. Garnish with coriander leaves and serve with steamed basmati rice.

**For creamy prawn & courgette curry**, replace the fish with 750 g (1½ lb) raw peeled tiger prawns and 2 courgettes, cut into 1 x 4 cm (½ x 1½ inch) batons. Cook as above, until the prawns turn pink and are cooked through and the courgette is just tender. Serve with steamed basmati rice.

# curried crab & prawn cakes

Serves **4**
Preparation time **10 minutes**, plus chilling
Cooking time **20–25 minutes**

400 g (13 oz) **fresh white crabmeat**
400 g (13 oz) **raw tiger prawns**, peeled and deveined
1 tablespoon **hot curry powder** (see page 16)
2 **garlic cloves**, crushed
1 teaspoon peeled and grated **fresh root ginger**
1 **fresh red chilli**, deseeded and finely chopped
4 tablespoons finely chopped **red onion**
8 tablespoons chopped **coriander leaves**, plus extra to garnish
1 **small egg**, beaten
100 g (3½ oz) **fresh wholemeal breadcrumbs**
**cooking oil spray**
**salt** and **pepper**
**lemon wedges**, to serve

**Place** the crabmeat, prawns, curry powder, garlic, ginger, chilli, onion, coriander, egg and breadcrumbs in a food processor. Season well and pulse for a few seconds until well mixed. Transfer to a bowl, cover and chill in the refrigerator for 5–6 hours or overnight.

**Preheat** the oven to 200°C (400°F), Gas Mark 6, line a baking sheet with greaseproof paper and spray with a little cooking oil spray.

**Divide** the crab mixture into 16 equal portions and shape each into a round cake. Arrange on the prepared baking sheet, spray with a little cooking oil spray and bake for 20–25 minutes until lightly browned and cooked through. Garnish with coriander and serve immediately with lemon wedges.

**For piquant crab, prawn & rice salad**, place 400g (13 oz) each of fresh white crabmeat and cooked peeled prawns in a salad bowl with 250 g (8 oz) cold cooked basmati rice. Add 6 finely sliced spring onions, ½ finely diced cucumber, 10 halved cherry tomatoes and a small handful of chopped coriander leaves. In a small bowl, whisk 3 tablespoons light olive oil with 4 tablespoons lemon juice, 1 teaspoon agave syrup and 1 finely chopped red chilli. Season, pour over the salad and toss to mix well.

# monkfish korma

Serves **4**
Preparation time **10 minutes**
Cooking time **20 minutes**

1 tablespoon **groundnut oil**
2 tablespoons **korma curry powder**
750 g (1½ lb) **monkfish fillet**, cubed
large bunch of **coriander leaves**, finely chopped
1 **red onion**, finely chopped
finely grated rind and juice of 2 **limes**
400 ml (14 fl oz) **reduced-fat coconut milk**
**salt** and **pepper**

**Heat** the oil in a wide saucepan over a medium heat. Add the curry powder and stir-fry for 20–30 seconds or until fragrant. Add the monkfish, coriander and red onion and cook, stirring, for a further 20–30 seconds.

**Add** the lime rind and juice and the coconut milk. Bring to the boil, reduce the heat and simmer for 15 minutes or until the fish is cooked through. Season to taste and serve immediately with steamed rice.

**For monkfish Madras**, replace the korma curry powder with Madras curry powder, and the coconut milk with 200 ml (7 fl oz) tomato passata and 200 ml (7 fl oz) fish stock. Cook as above until the fish is cooked through. Serve with warmed naan bread or chapatis.

# red fish, broccoli & bean curry

Serves **4**
Preparation time **15 minutes**
Cooking time **10 minutes**

1 tablespoon **groundnut oil**
1½–2 tablespoons **Thai red curry paste** (see page 17)
200 ml (7 fl oz) **coconut cream**
250 ml (8 fl oz) **vegetable stock**
1 tablespoon **tamarind paste**
1 tablespoon **Thai fish sauce**
1 tablespoon **palm sugar** or **brown sugar**
200 g (7 oz) **broccoli florets**
200 g (7 oz) **French beans**, cut into 2.5 cm (1 inch) lengths
450 g (14½ oz) thick **white fish fillet**, skinned and cubed
150 g (5 oz) can **bamboo shoots**, drained (optional)
small handful of **Thai basil leaves**, to garnish
**lime wedges**, to serve

**Heat** the oil in a large wok or frying pan over a medium heat, add the curry paste and stir-fry for 1–2 minutes. Stir in the coconut cream, stock, tamarind paste, fish sauce and sugar and bring to the boil, then reduce the heat and simmer gently for a further 2–3 minutes.

**Add** the broccoli and beans and simmer gently for 2 minutes. Stir in the fish and simmer gently for a further 3–4 minutes or until just cooked through. Stir in the bamboo shoots, if using.

**Ladle** into warmed bowls, sprinkle with Thai basil and serve with lime wedges.

**For Thai mixed seafood curry**, replace the broccoli and French beans with 1 large thinly sliced carrot and 1 thinly sliced red pepper. Follow the recipe above, omitting the fish, but adding 12 raw king prawns, peeled and deveined, 125 g (4 oz) prepared squid rings and 500 g (1 lb) scrubbed and debearded mussels. Simmer gently until the mussels open, discarding any that do not. Add 200 g (7 oz) fresh or canned pineapple chunks instead of the bamboo shoots and serve as above.

# sweet & sour salmon curry

Serves **4**
Preparation time **15 minutes**
Cooking time **20 minutes**

1 tablespoon **Thai fish sauce**
1 teaspoon **palm sugar** or
   **brown sugar**
2 **lemon grass stalks**, bruised
600 ml (1 pint) **water**
2 tablespoons **lemon juice**
1 tablespoon **tamarind paste**
200 g (7 oz) **pineapple,** cubed
4 **salmon fillets**, about 200 g
   (7 oz) each, skinned

**Curry paste**
2 **garlic cloves**, peeled
5 **dried red chillies**
large pinch of **sea salt**
1 teaspoon **ground turmeric**
2 tablespoons finely chopped
   **lemon grass** (tough outer
   leaves removed)
1 tablespoon **shrimp paste**

**Place** all the ingredients for the curry paste in a mini blender and blend until smooth, adding a little water if necessary. Transfer the paste to a wide saucepan and add the fish sauce, sugar, lemon grass stalks and two-thirds of the measured water. Bring to the boil, reduce the heat and simmer for 8–10 minutes.

**Mix** the lemon juice with the tamarind paste and remaining water. Add to the saucepan with the pineapple and stir to mix well. Add the salmon fillets and simmer gently for 8–10 minutes until cooked through. Remove from the heat and serve immediately with steamed jasmine rice.

**For quick Thai red cod curry,** lightly spray a large frying pan with cooking oil spray and stir-fry 2 finely chopped garlic cloves, 4 finely sliced shallots, 2 teaspoons grated fresh root ginger and 2 tablespoons Thai red curry paste (see page 17) for 2–3 minutes. Add 400 ml (14 fl oz) reduced-fat coconut milk, 1 teaspoon agave syrup and 200 ml (7 fl oz) fish stock and bring to the boil. Add 750 g (1½ lb) cubed cod fillet and cook for 5–6 minutes or until cooked through. Remove from the heat and serve immediately with steamed jasmine rice.

# curry leaf & tomato prawns

Serves **4**
Preparation time **15 minutes**
Cooking time **15–20 minutes**

1 tablespoon **groundnut oil**
10–12 **curry leaves**
2 **large shallots**, halved and
    finely sliced
2 teaspoons finely grated
    **garlic**
1 teaspoon peeled and finely
    grated **fresh root ginger**
1 tablespoon **fennel seeds**
1 tablespoon **medium curry
    powder** (see page 16)
6 **large ripe tomatoes**,
    peeled, deseeded and
    chopped
750 g (1½ lb) **raw tiger
    prawns**, peeled and
    deveined
**salt**

**Heat** the oil in a large wok or frying pan over a medium heat. Add the curry leaves and stir-fry for 30 seconds. Add the shallots and stir-fry for a further 4–5 minutes.

**Add** the garlic, ginger and fennel seeds, reduce the heat and cook gently for 2–3 minutes. Sprinkle over the curry powder and add the tomatoes, including any juices. Increase the heat and stir-fry for 3–4 minutes.

**Add** the prawns and continue cooking over a high heat for 6–7 minutes until the prawns turn pink and are just cooked through. Remove from the heat, season to taste and serve immediately with rice or crushed sesame spiced potatoes.

**For crushed sesame spiced potatoes**, to serve as an accompaniment, peel 4 medium potatoes and cut into 1 cm (½ inch) dice. Boil for 12 minutes or until just tender, then drain thoroughly. Heat 1 tablespoon groundnut oil in a large frying pan over a high heat. Add 1 tablespoon sesame seeds, 2 teaspoons cumin seeds, 2 teaspoons red chilli powder, ¼ teaspoon ground turmeric and the potatoes and stir-fry for 6–8 minutes, crushing them lightly with the back of a spoon. Season and serve.

# monkfish tikka kebabs

Serves **4**
Preparation time **15 minutes**,
  plus marinating
Cooking time **8–10 minutes**

750 g (1 ½ lb) **monkfish fillet**,
  cubed
2 **red peppers**, cored,
  deseeded and cubed
2 **yellow peppers**, cored,
  deseeded and cubed
**salt** and **pepper**
chopped **coriander** and **mint
  leaves**, to garnish
**lime wedges**, to serve

**Tikka marinade**
350 ml (12 fl oz) **fat-free
  natural yogurt**
2 tablespoons finely grated
  **onion**
1 tablespoon finely grated
  **garlic**
1 tablespoon peeled and finely
  grated **fresh root ginger**
juice of 2 **limes**
3 tablespoons **tikka curry
  powder**

**Mix** all the marinade ingredients in a large bowl.
Add the fish and peppers, season well and toss to
coat evenly. Cover and marinate in the refrigerator for
1–2 hours.

**Preheat** a grill or barbecue until hot. Thread the
fish and peppers on to 8 metal skewers and grill for
4–5 minutes on each side until the fish is just cooked
through. Serve immediately, garnished with chopped
coriander and mint, with lime wedges for squeezing.

**For monkfish tikka wraps**, cook the fish and
peppers as above and remove from the skewers. Warm
8 medium chapatis or corn tortillas and top each one
with a small handful of shredded lettuce. Divide the fish
and peppers between them, drizzle each with a little fat-
free fromage frais, wrap up and serve.

# simple fish & potato curry

Serves **4**

Preparation time **20 minutes**

Cooking time **40 minutes**

40 g (1½ oz) fresh **root ginger**, peeled and grated

1 teaspoon **ground turmeric**

2 **garlic cloves**, crushed

2 teaspoons **medium curry paste**

150 ml (¼ pint) **fat-free natural yogurt**

625 g (1¼ lb) **white fish fillet**, skinned and cubed

2 tablespoons **groundnut oil**

1 large **onion**, sliced

1 **cinnamon stick**, halved

2 teaspoons **palm sugar** or **brown suga**r

2 **bay leaves**

400 g (13 oz) can **chopped tomatoes**

300 ml (½ pint) **fish stock**

500 g (1 lb) **waxy potatoes**, cubed

small handful of chopped **coriander leaves**

**salt** and **pepper**

**Mix** the ginger with the turmeric, garlic and curry paste in a large bowl. Stir in the yogurt until well combined, then add the fish and toss to coat in the spice mixture.

**Heat** the oil in a large saucepan and gently fry the onion, cinnamon, sugar and bay leaves until the onion is soft. Add the tomatoes, stock and potatoes and bring to the boil. Cook, uncovered, for about 20 minutes until the potatoes are tender and the sauce has thickened.

**Add** the fish and spicy yogurt and reduce the heat to its lowest setting. Cook gently for about 10 minutes or until the fish is cooked through. Season to taste and stir in the coriander before serving.

**For homemade fish stock**, melt a knob of butter in a large saucepan and gently fry 2 roughly chopped shallots, 1 small roughly chopped leek and 1 roughly chopped celery stick or fennel bulb. Add 1 kg (2 lb) white fish bones, heads and trimmings, or prawn shells, several parsley sprigs, ½ lemon and 1 teaspoon peppercorns. Cover with cold water and bring to a simmer. Cook, uncovered, on the lowest setting for 30 minutes. Strain through a sieve and leave to cool.

# singapore curried scallops

Serves **4**

Preparation time **10 minutes**

Cooking time **5 minutes**

24 fresh **king scallops**

3 tablespoons **mild curry powder** (see page 16)

1 tablespoon **groundnut oil**

4 tablespoons **light soy sauce**

2 tablespoons **rice wine**

2 **fresh red chillies**, finely sliced

7 cm (3 inch) piece of **fresh root ginger**, peeled and finely shredded

6 **spring onions**, finely sliced

**salt** and **pepper**

**Place** the scallops on a plate, dust the curry powder over them and lightly season to taste. Toss to mix well.

**Heat** the oil in a large nonstick frying pan. When it is very hot, add the scallops, spacing them out around the pan. Sear for 1–2 minutes on each side, then remove from the pan and arrange on a warmed serving platter.

**Mix** together the soy sauce and wine and sprinkle over the scallops. Scatter a little chilli, ginger and spring onion over each one, and serve immediately with egg-fried rice.

**For mild scallop & coconut curry**, heat 1 tablespoon groundnut oil in a large frying pan and add 1 finely chopped onion, 1 deseeded and finely chopped red chilli, 2 finely chopped garlic cloves and 1 teaspoon very finely diced ginger. Stir-fry for 3–4 minutes or until the onion has just softened, then add 1 tablespoon mild curry powder (see page 16) and stir-fry for 1 minute. Add 400 ml (14 fl oz) reduced-fat coconut milk and 200 ml (7 fl oz) tomato passata and bring to the boil. Reduce the heat to medium, and cook for 6–8 minutes, stirring often. Season to taste, stir in 24 fresh king scallops and cook for 4–5 minutes or until they are just cooked through. Remove from the heat and serve in warmed bowls with rice.

# yellow salmon curry

Serves **4**
Preparation time **15 minutes**
Cooking time **25–30 minutes**

3 **garlic cloves**, finely grated
2 **fresh green chillies**,
    deseeded and finely
    chopped
2 teaspoons peeled and finely
    grated **fresh root ginger**
1 tablespoon **groundnut oil**
1 **onion**, finely chopped
1 tablespoon **ground turmeric**
200 ml (7 fl oz) **reduced-fat**
    **coconut milk**
200 ml (7 fl oz) **water**
2 **potatoes**, peeled and diced
4 thick **salmon steaks**, about
    200 g (7 oz) each
2 **tomatoes**, roughly chopped
**salt**
chopped **coriander leaves**, to
    garnish

**Pound** the garlic, chillies and ginger with a pestle and mortar until you have a smooth paste.

**Heat** the oil in a large nonstick wok or saucepan over a medium heat. Add the paste and stir-fry for 2–3 minutes, then add the onion and turmeric. Stir-fry for a further 2–3 minutes until fragrant.

**Stir** in the coconut milk, measured water and the potatoes. Bring to the boil, reduce the heat to low and simmer gently for 10–12 minutes, stirring occasionally.

**Season** the fish with salt and add to the pan with the tomatoes. Bring the mixture back to the boil and simmer gently for 6–8 minutes until the fish is cooked through. Remove from the heat and garnish with chopped coriander. Serve hot with steamed white rice.

**For yellow mussel curry**, replace the salmon with 1 kg (2 lb) mussels, which have been scrubbed and debearded. Cover the pan and cook over a high heat for 6–8 minutes or until the mussels have opened, discarding any that do not. Remove from the heat, garnish with chopped coriander and serve hot with crusty bread.

# spicy cod & tomato curry

Serves **4**
Preparation time **15 minutes**
Cooking time **40–50 minutes**

60 ml (2½ fl oz) **lemon juice**
60 ml (2½ fl oz) **rice wine
  vinegar**
2 tablespoons **cumin seeds**
2 tablespoons **hot curry
  powder** (see page 16)
large pinch of **salt**
750 g (1½ lb) thick **cod fillet**,
  skinned and cubed
1 tablespoon **groundnut oil**
1 **onion**, finely chopped
3 **garlic cloves**, finely chopped
2 teaspoons peeled and finely
  grated **fresh root ginger**
2 x 400 g (13 oz) cans
  **chopped tomatoes**
1 teaspoon **agave syrup**

**Mix** the lemon juice with the vinegar, cumin seeds, curry powder and salt in a shallow non-metallic bowl. Add the fish and turn to coat evenly. Cover and marinate in the refrigerator for 25–30 minutes.

**Meanwhile,** heat a wok or large frying pan with a lid over a high heat and add the oil. When the oil is hot, add the onion, garlic and ginger. Reduce the heat and cook gently for 10 minutes, stirring occasionally.

**Add** the tomatoes and agave syrup, stir well and bring to the boil. Reduce the heat, cover and cook gently for 15–20 minutes, stirring occasionally.

**Add** the fish and its marinade, and stir gently to mix. Cover and simmer gently for 15–20 minutes until the fish is cooked through. Ladle into shallow bowls and serve with steamed basmati rice.

**For cod & tomato biryani**, place 1 tablespoon medium curry powder (see page 16) in a medium saucepan with 1 bay leaf, 1 cinnamon stick, a large pinch of saffron, 4 crushed cardamom pods, 3 cloves, 6 tablespoons tomato purée and 300 g (10 oz) basmati rice. Pour in 650 ml (1 pint 2 fl oz) hot fish stock, season and stir to mix well. Bring back to the boil and gently stir in 400 g (13 oz) skinless cod fillet chunks. Reduce the heat to low, cover the pan and cook gently for 10–12 minutes or until all the liquid has been absorbed. Remove from the heat and allow to stand, covered and undisturbed, for 10–15 minutes. Fluff up the grains with a fork and serve.

# kerala mackerel curry

Serves **4**

Preparation time **10 minutes**, plus soaking

Cooking time **15–20 minutes**

4 **dried Kashmiri chillies**, soaked in hot water for 30 minutes

1 tablespoon **paprika**

2 tablespoons **mild curry powder** (see page 16)

150 g (5 oz) **fresh coconut, grated**

200 ml (7 fl oz) **reduced-fat coconut milk**

200 ml (7 fl oz) **water**

2 tablespoons **tamarind paste**

2 **fresh green chillies**, halved lengthways

1 tablespoon peeled and finely grated **fresh root ginger**

1 small **onion**, finely chopped

750 g (1½ lb) **mackerel fillets**

**salt**

**Place** the soaked chillies, paprika, curry powder and coconut in a food processor with the coconut milk and blend to a smooth paste.

**Transfer** the spice paste to a wide saucepan, add the measured water, stir to mix well and bring to a gentle simmer over a medium-low heat. Add the tamarind paste, green chillies, ginger and onion, and season to taste. Stir and simmer for 2–3 minutes.

**Add** the fish to the pan, stir once, cover and simmer gently for 10–15 minutes until the fish is just cooked. Serve hot with steamed rice.

**For grilled spiced mackerel**, arrange 8 mackerel fillets on a lightly greased grill rack, skin side up. Make 3–4 diagonal slashes in each fillet. Mix together 2 tablespoons medium curry powder (see page 16), 4 tablespoons lemon juice, 2 teaspoons each of crushed garlic and ginger, and 2 tablespoons coconut cream. Season and spread this mixture over the fish. Cook under a medium-hot grill for 8–10 minutes or until cooked through. Serve immediately.

# spicy crab curry

Serves **4**
Preparation time **15 minutes**
Cooking time **40 minutes**

2 **cooked fresh crabs**, about
750 g (1½ lb) each
3 **onions**, finely chopped
6 **garlic cloves**, finely chopped
1 tablespoon peeled and finely
grated **fresh root ginger**
½ teaspoon **fenugreek seeds**
10 **curry leaves**
1 **cinnamon stick**
2 teaspoons **chilli powder**
1 teaspoon **ground turmeric**
400 ml (14 fl oz) **reduced-fat
coconut milk**
**salt** and **pepper**

**Divide** each crab into portions, by first removing the main shell. Next remove the two large claws and use a sharp knife to cut the body into 2 pieces, leaving the legs attached.

**Place** the onion, garlic, ginger, fenugreek, curry leaves, cinnamon, chilli, turmeric and coconut milk in a large saucepan. Season to taste, cover and simmer gently for 30 minutes.

**Add** the crabs to the simmering sauce and cook for 10 minutes to heat through. Serve immediately, with plenty of napkins.

**For spicy crab with angel hair pasta**, cook 375 g (12 oz) angel hair pasta according to packet instructions. Meanwhile, heat 1 tablespoon groundnut oil in a large frying pan over a gentle heat and add 3 finely chopped garlic cloves, 1 finely chopped red chilli, 6 finely chopped spring onions, 6 tablespoons reduced-fat coconut milk and 400 g (13 oz) white crab meat. Season and stir-fry for 3–4 minutes. Drain the pasta and add to the crab mixture. Toss to mix well and serve immediately.

# sri lankan scallop curry

Serves **4**

Preparation time **10 minutes**

Cooking time **20–25 minutes**

1 tablespoon **groundnut oil**

¼ teaspoon **turmeric**

1 teaspoon **cumin seeds**

2 **fresh red chillies**, deseeded and chopped

1 **onion**, finely chopped

6 **tomatoes**, peeled, deseeded and diced

3 tablespoons **medium curry powder** (see page 16)

1 tablespoon **coconut cream**

1 teaspoon **ground cumin**

1 teaspoon **garam masala**

400 g (13 oz) fresh **king scallops**

small handful of finely chopped **coriander leaves**

**salt** and **pepper**

**Heat** the oil in a frying pan over a low heat. Add the turmeric, cumin seeds and chillies, and fry briefly to release the flavours. Add the onion and cook gently for 10 minutes until softened but not coloured.

**Stir** in the tomatoes and curry powder and simmer for 5 minutes or until the tomatoes have cooked down to a thick sauce. Stir in the coconut cream, ground cumin and garam masala and season to taste.

**Add** the scallops and cook for a few minutes until the scallops are just cooked through. Check the seasoning and adjust if necessary. Stir in the coriander and serve immediately.

**For homemade garam masala**, place 4 tablespoons coriander seeds, 2 tablespoons cumin seeds, 1 tablespoon black peppercorns, 1 tablespoon ground ginger, 1 teaspoon cardamom seeds, 4 cloves, 1 cinnamon stick and 1 crushed dried bay leaf in a frying pan. Dry-roast over a medium-low heat for a few minutes until fragrant. Remove from the heat and allow to cool. Tip the contents of the pan into a mini blender or clean electric coffee grinder, and grind to a fine powder. Store in an airtight container for up to 1 month, or in the refrigerator for up to 3 months.

# mango & prawn curry

Serves **4**
Preparation time **10 minutes**
Cooking time **20–25 minutes**

3 **garlic cloves**, crushed
2 teaspoons peeled and finely
　grated **fresh root ginger**
2 tablespoons **ground
　coriander**
2 teaspoons **ground cumin**
1 teaspoon **chilli powder**
1 teaspoon **paprika**
½ teaspoon **ground turmeric**
1 tablespoon **palm sugar** or
　**brown sugar**
400 ml (14 fl oz) **water**
1 **green mango**, peeled,
　stoned and thinly sliced
400 ml (14 fl oz) **reduced-fat
　coconut milk**
1 tablespoon **tamarind paste**
625 g (1¼ lb) **raw tiger
　prawns**, peeled and
　deveined
small bunch of **fresh
　coriander**
**salt**

**Place** the garlic, ginger, ground coriander, cumin, chilli powder, paprika, turmeric and sugar in a large wok or frying pan. Pour in the measured water and stir to mix well. Bring to the boil, reduce the heat and cook, covered, for 8–10 minutes.

**Add** the mango, coconut milk and tamarind paste and stir to combine. Bring the mixture back to the boil, then add the prawns. Reduce the heat and simmer gently for 6–8 minutes.

**Tear** half of the coriander leaves into the curry and cook for another 2 minutes until the prawns have turned pink and are just cooked through. Season to taste and serve immediately with steamed basmati rice, garnished with the remaining coriander.

**For chicken & sweet potato curry**, simmer the spices in the measured water as above. Omit the mango and prawns and add 1 small peeled and diced sweet potato and 500 g (1 lb) diced skinless chicken breast fillets with the coconut milk and tamarind paste. Bring to the boil, reduce the heat and simmer gently for 20 minutes until the chicken is cooked through. Add the coriander and serve as above.

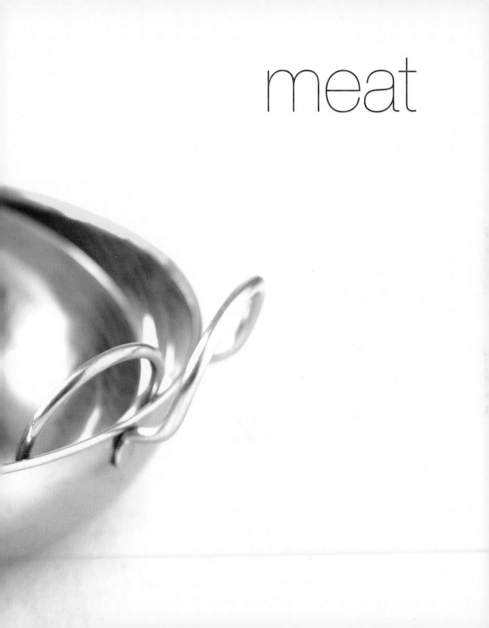

meat

# beef & potato madras

Serves **4**

Preparation time **15 minutes**,
  plus marinating

Cooking time **2–3 hours**

5 tablespoons **fat-free natural
  yogurt**

5 tablespoons **Madras curry
  powder**

625 g (1¼ lb) **lean beef fillet**,
  cubed

2 tablespoons **groundnut oil**

1 large **onion**, thinly sliced

3 **garlic cloves**, crushed

1 teaspoon peeled and finely
  grated **fresh root ginger**

2 **potatoes**, peeled and cut
  into 2.5 cm (1 inch) chunks

400 g (13 oz) can **chopped
  tomatoes**

400 ml (14 fl oz) **beef stock**

¼ teaspoon **garam masala**

**salt**

chopped **coriander leaves**,
  to garnish

**Mix** the yogurt with the curry powder in a large non-metallic bowl. Add the meat, toss to combine, season to taste and marinate in the refrigerator for 24 hours.

**Heat** the oil in a large nonstick wok or frying pan with a lid over a medium heat. Add the onion and stir-fry for 4–5 minutes until soft. Add the garlic and ginger, and stir-fry for a further 30 seconds.

**Reduce** the heat to low and add the marinated meat. Stir-fry for 10–15 minutes. Add the potatoes, tomatoes and stock and bring to the boil. Reduce the heat to very low (using a heat diffuser if possible), cover the pan tightly and simmer gently for 1½–2 hours, stirring occasionally, until the meat is meltingly tender. Check the seasoning and adjust if necessary. Serve garnished with chopped coriander.

**For homemade Madras curry powder**, dry-roast 8 tablespoons coriander seeds, 6 tablespoons cumin seeds, 1 tablespoon black mustard seeds and 1 tablespoon fennel seeds in a nonstick frying pan over a low heat until they begin to 'pop'. Add 4 tablespoons ground cinnamon, 8 tablespoons black peppercorns, 1 teaspoon grated nutmeg, 1 tablespoon cloves, 2 tablespoons ground cardamom, 2 tablespoons ground turmeric, 2 tablespoons ground ginger and 2 tablespoons hot chilli powder. Continue to heat and stir gently for 2 minutes. Allow to cool, tip the contents of the pan into a mini blender or clean electric coffee grinder, and grind to a fine powder. Store in an airtight container for up to 1 month, or in the refrigerator for up to 3 months.

# pork & lemon grass curry

Serves **4**
Preparation time **20 minutes**
Cooking time **about 1 hour**

1 tablespoon **groundnut oil**
6 **shallots**, finely chopped
1 **fresh red chilli**, thinly sliced
2 teaspoons peeled and finely
   grated **galangal**
6 tablespoons finely chopped
   **lemon grass** (tough outer
   leaves removed)
2 teaspoons finely grated
   **garlic**
2 teaspoons crushed
   **fenugreek seeds**
1 tablespoon **ground cumin**
1 teaspoon **ground turmeric**
1 tablespoon **tamarind paste**
finely grated rind and juice of
   **1 lime**
400 ml (14 fl oz) **reduced-fat
   coconut milk**
400 ml (14 fl oz) **chicken
   stock**
12 baby **new potatoes**
2 **red peppers**, cored,
   deseeded and cubed
625 g (1¼lb) lean **pork fillet**,
   cubed
**salt** and **pepper**

**Heat** the oil in a large nonstick wok or frying pan over a medium-high heat. Add the shallots, chilli, galangal, lemon grass, garlic, fenugreek seeds, cumin and turmeric, and stir-fry for 2–3 minutes until soft and fragrant.

**Stir** in the tamarind, lime rind and juice, coconut milk, stock, potatoes and red pepper, and bring to the boil. Reduce the heat and simmer, covered, for 25 minutes, stirring occasionally.

**Add** the pork and season to taste. Simmer gently, uncovered, for 25–30 minutes or until tender. Ladle into warmed bowls and serve with rice.

**For curried pork & lemon grass patties**, place 750 g (1½ lb) minced pork in a large bowl with 1 chopped red chilli, 4 sliced spring onions, the grated rind and juice of 1 lime, 1 tablespoon soy sauce, 2 tablespoons lemon grass paste and 4 tablespoons chopped coriander leaves. Add enough beaten egg, about 1 large egg, to bring it all together. Shape into 8 patties and arrange on a plate lined with greaseproof paper. Cover and chill for 3–4 hours or overnight. Transfer the patties to a grill rack, spray with cooking oil spray and cook under a preheated grill for 6–8 minutes on each side or until cooked through.

# pea & lamb korma

Serves **4**
Preparation time **10 minutes**
Cooking time **30 minutes**

2 tablespoons **groundnut oil**
1 **onion**, chopped
2 **garlic cloves**, crushed
250 g (8 oz) **potatoes**, diced
500 g (1 lb) **minced lamb**
1 tablespoon **korma curry powder**
200 g (7 oz) fresh or frozen **peas**
200 ml (7 fl oz) **vegetable stock**
2 tablespoons **mango chutney**
**salt** and **pepper**
chopped **coriander leaves**, to garnish

**Heat** the oil in a large saucepan, add the onion and garlic and cook for 5 minutes until the onion is soft and starting to brown. Add the potatoes and lamb and cook, stirring and breaking up the mince with a wooden spoon, for 5 minutes or until the meat has browned.

**Add** the curry powder and cook, stirring, for 1 minute. Add the remaining ingredients and season to taste. Bring to the boil, reduce the heat, cover tightly and simmer for 20 minutes.

**Garnish** with coriander and serve with natural yogurt and chapatis.

**For spicy Indian wraps**, finely shred 200 g (7 oz) iceberg lettuce and toss in a bowl with 1 coarsely grated carrot. Heat 8 large flour tortillas on a griddle pan for 1–2 minutes on each side and then pile some of the lettuce mixture on the centre of each. Divide the korma mixture (cooked as above) between the wraps and roll up to enclose the filling. Serve with natural yogurt.

# slow-cooked aromatic pork curry

Serves **4**
Preparation time **10 minutes**
Cooking time **2½–3 hours**

750 g (1 ½ lb) **pork belly**,
  trimmed and cubed
400 ml (14 fl oz) **chicken
  stock**
75 ml (3 fl oz) **light soy sauce**
finely grated rind and juice of
  1 large **orange**
1 tablespoon peeled and finely
  shredded **fresh root ginger**
2 **garlic cloves**, sliced
1 dried **red Kashmiri chilli**
2 tablespoons **medium curry
  powder** (see page 18)
1 tablespoon **hot chilli
  powder**
1 tablespoon **dark
  muscovado sugar**
3 **cinnamon sticks**
3 **cloves**
10 **black peppercorns**
2–3 **star anise**
**salt**

**Place** the pork in a large saucepan or casserole, cover with water and bring to the boil over a high heat. Cover, reduce the heat and simmer gently for 30 minutes. Drain and return the pork to the pan with the remaining ingredients. Season to taste.

**Add** just enough water to cover the pork and bring to the boil over a high heat. Cover tightly, reduce the heat to low and cook very gently for 1 ½ hours, stirring occasionally.

**Remove** the lid and simmer, uncovered, for 30 minutes, stirring occasionally, until the meat is meltingly tender. Serve with steamed Asian greens and rice.

### For slow-cooked aromatic lamb curry, heat
1 tablespoon groundnut oil in a large saucepan over a high heat. Add 750 g (1 ½ lb) lean cubed lamb and brown for 4–5 minutes. Stir in 1 roughly chopped onion, 4 sliced garlic cloves, 2 teaspoons grated ginger, 2 dried red Kashmiri chillies, 1 cinnamon stick, 1 star anise, 4 green cardamom pods and 2 tablespoons mild curry powder (see page 16). Stir-fry for 2–3 minutes and then add 4 peeled, deseeded and roughly chopped tomatoes and 750 ml (1 ¼ pints) lamb or chicken stock. Bring to the boil, cover and gently cook for 1 ½ hours or until the lamb is meltingly tender. Serve with steamed rice.

# fragrant vietnamese beef curry

Serves **4**

Preparation time **15 minutes**

Cooking time **20–25 minutes**

2 tablespoons **groundnut oil**

750 g (1½ lb) thin-cut **fillet steak**, cut into strips

1 **onion**, finely sliced

4 **garlic cloves**, crushed

1 **fresh red chilli**, finely sliced

2 **star anise**

1 teaspoon **cardamom seeds**, crushed

1 **cinnamon stick**

300 g (10 oz) **French beans**, trimmed

1 **carrot**, cut into batons

2 tablespoons **Thai fish sauce**

2 tablespoons **ground bean sauce**

**To garnish**

small handful of finely chopped **coriander leaves**

small handful of finely chopped **mint leaves**

**Heat** half the oil in a large nonstick frying pan and stir-fry the beef in batches for 1–2 minutes. Remove with a slotted spoon and keep warm.

**Heat** the remaining oil in the frying pan and stir-fry the onion for 4–5 minutes until softened, then add the garlic, chilli, star anise, cardamom, cinnamon, beans and carrot. Stir-fry for 6–8 minutes.

**Return** the beef to the pan with the fish sauce and ground bean sauce. Stir-fry for 3–4 minutes or until heated through. Remove from the heat and sprinkle over the chopped herbs just before serving.

**For fresh beef spring rolls**, soak 8 large rice paper wrappers in warm water for 3–4 minutes or until soft and pliable. Pat dry with kitchen paper and spread out on a clean work surface. Thinly shred 6 iceberg lettuce leaves and divide between the wrappers. Top each with 3 tablespoons of the beef curry, cooked as above, arranged in a neat pile along the middles of the wrappers. Turn up the bottom of the wrapper to cover the filling then carefully turn the two sides in and very gently roll up. Transfer to a serving plate and cover with a damp cloth while you make the remaining rolls. Serve immediately or the wrappers will dry out and become tough.

# spicy marinated lamb chops

Serves **4**

Preparation time **10 minutes**, plus marinating

Cooking time **8–10 minutes**

12 **lamb chops**

125 ml (4 fl oz) **fat-free natural yogurt**

4 tablespoons **tomato purée**

4 tablespoons **medium curry paste**

1 teaspoon grated **garlic**

1 teaspoon peeled and finely grated **fresh root ginger**

large pinch of **sea salt**

3 tablespoons **lemon juice**

**To serve**

1 **red onion**, sliced

4 **tomatoes**, sliced

½ **cucumber**, sliced

**Arrange** the chops in a single layer in a shallow non-metallic dish. Mix the yogurt with the tomato purée, curry paste, garlic, ginger, sea salt and lemon juice, and rub into the lamb. Cover and marinate in the refrigerator for 4–5 hours or overnight.

**Preheat** the oven to 220°C (425°F), Gas Mark 7, and line a large roasting tin with foil. Arrange the chops in a single layer in the tin and cook in the preheated oven for 8–10 minutes, turning halfway through cooking, or until the lamb is cooked to your liking. Serve immediately with onion rings and tomato and cucumber slices.

**For spicy beef skewers**, cut 750 g (1 ½ lb) lean beef fillet into large cubes and place in a non-metallic dish. Mix together the marinade as above and pour over the beef. Toss to mix well and marinate in the refrigerator for 6–8 hours or overnight. When ready to cook, thread the marinated beef on to 8 metal skewers and grill under a medium-hot grill for 3–4 minutes on each side or until cooked to your liking. Serve with warm naan breads and cucumber & mint raita (see page 200).

# curried veal pie

Serves **4**
Preparation time **10 minutes**
Cooking time **1 hour**

**cooking oil spray**
500 g (1 lb) **minced veal**
1 large **onion**, finely chopped
2 **garlic cloves**, crushed
2 tablespoons **hot curry powder** (see page 16)
3 tablespoons **mango chutney**
200 g (7 oz) fresh or frozen **peas**
1 large **carrot**, finely diced
50 g (2 oz) **sultanas**
400 ml (14 fl oz) **fat-free natural yogurt**
4 large **eggs**
large handful of finely chopped **coriander leaves**
**salt** and **pepper**

**Preheat** the oven to 180°C (350°F), Gas Mark 4. Spray a large nonstick frying pan with cooking oil spray and place over a medium heat. Add the veal and stir-fry for 2–3 minutes, stirring constantly, until the meat changes colour. Add the onion and cook for a further 4–5 minutes, stirring occasionally, until the onion starts to soften and the veal is lightly browned.

**Add** the garlic and curry powder, and fry for 1–2 minutes to allow the spices to cook. Remove the pan from the heat and stir in the mango chutney, peas, carrot and sultanas.

**Spoon** the mixture into a shallow ovenproof dish and press down well with the back of a spoon. Whisk the yogurt with the eggs, stir in the chopped coriander and season to taste. Pour over the meat to cover evenly. Cook in the preheated oven for 45–50 minutes until the mixture is piping hot and the top is set and golden. Serve with a crisp green salad.

**For spicy veal & pea curry**, spray a large saucepan with cooking oil spray and add 1 finely chopped onion. Cook over a low heat for 15–20 minutes until soft. Add 2 teaspoons each of grated garlic and fresh root ginger, 2 finely sliced red chillies, 1 tablespoon cumin seeds and 2 tablespoons hot curry paste and stir-fry over a high heat for 1–2 minutes. Add 750 g (1½ lb) minced veal and stir-fry for 3–4 minutes, then add a 400 g (13 oz) can chopped tomatoes, 1 teaspoon agave syrup and 4 tablespoons tomato purée and bring to the boil. Season, cover and cook gently for 1½ hours. Ten minutes before the end of cooking, add 2 tablespoons coconut cream and 200 g (7 oz) peas. Serve with rice.

# goan pork vindaloo

Serves **4**

Preparation time **25 minutes**,
   plus marinating

Cooking time **1 hour
   40 minutes**

2 teaspoons **cumin seeds**,
   dry-roasted

6 dried **red chillies**

1 teaspoon **cardamom seeds**,
   crushed

1 **cinnamon stick**

10 **black peppercorns**

8 **garlic cloves**, crushed

5 tablespoons **wine vinegar**

625 g (1 ¼ lb) **boneless pork**,
   cubed

1 tablespoon **groundnut oil**

1 **onion**, finely chopped

2 tablespoons **hot curry
   powder** (see page 16)

4 **potatoes**, peeled and
   quartered

6 tablespoons **tomato purée**

1 tablespoon **sugar**

400 g (13 oz) can **chopped
   tomatoes**

200 ml (7 fl oz) **chicken stock**

**salt** and **pepper**

**Place** the cumin, chillies, cardamom, cinnamon, peppercorns, garlic and vinegar into a mini blender and blend to a smooth paste. Place the pork in a non-metallic dish and pour over the paste. Rub into the pork, cover and marinate in the refrigerator for up to 24 hours.

**Heat** the oil in a large saucepan and add the onion. Stir-fry for 3–4 minutes, then add the curry powder and pork. Stir-fry for 3–4 minutes then stir in the potatoes, tomato purée, sugar, chopped tomatoes and stock.

**Season** and bring to the boil. Cover tightly and reduce the heat to low. Simmer for 1 ½ hours or until the pork is tender. Serve immediately with steamed white rice.

**For papaya and mint raita**, to serve as an accompaniment, mix 200 ml (7 fl oz) fat-free natural yogurt with a handful of chopped mint leaves. Halve, deseed and peel 1 small papaya, then dice the flesh and mix into the minted yogurt.

# caribbean lamb stoba

Serves **4**
Preparation time **25 minutes**
Cooking time **1¾ hours**

2 tablespoons **groundnut oil**
750 g (1 ½ lb) **lean lamb**,
　cubed
2 **onions**, finely chopped
2 teaspoons finely grated
　**fresh root ginger**
1 **scotch bonnet chilli**, thinly
　sliced
1 **red pepper**, cored,
　deseeded and roughly
　chopped
2 teaspoons **ground allspice**
3 teaspoons **ground cumin**
1 **cinnamon stick**
pinch of grated **nutmeg**
400 g (13 oz) can **chopped**
　**tomatoes**
300 g (10 oz) **cherry**
　**tomatoes**
finely grated rind and juice of
　2 **limes**
65 g (2½ oz) **soft brown**
　**sugar**
200 g (7 oz) fresh or frozen
　**peas**
**salt** and **pepper**

**Heat** half the oil in a large saucepan. Brown the lamb in batches for 3–4 minutes. Remove with a slotted spoon and set aside.

**Heat** the remaining oil in the saucepan and add the onion, ginger, chilli, red pepper and spices. Stir-fry for 3–4 minutes then add the lamb with the canned and cherry tomatoes, lime rind and juice, and sugar. Season and bring to the boil. Reduce the heat, cover tightly and simmer gently for 1½ hours or until the lamb is tender.

**Stir** in the peas 5 minutes before serving on warmed plates with rice.

### For Caribbean lamb, sweet potato & okra stoba,
add 500 g (1 lb) sweet potato, peeled and cubed, after 30 minutes of cooking. Fry 250 g (8 oz) okra, trimmed and thickly sliced, over a medium-high heat for about 5 minutes, or until lightly browned but still tender. Add the okra with the peas and finish as above.

# calf's liver curry

Serves **4**
Preparation time **10 minutes**
Cooking time **about**
   **40 minutes**

500 g (1 lb) **calf's liver,** thinly
   sliced
10 **black peppercorns**
1 tablespoon **groundnut oil**
1 fresh **red chilli**, finely
   chopped
1 **onion**, finely chopped
3 **garlic cloves**, finely chopped
1 teaspoon peeled and finely
   chopped **fresh root ginger**
1 tablespoon **hot curry
   powder** (see page 16)
6 tablespoons finely chopped
   **lemon grass** (tough outer
   leaves removed)
¼ teaspoon **ground cloves**
1 teaspoon **ground cinnamon**
10 **curry leaves**
1 tablespoon **white wine
   vinegar**
500 ml (17 fl oz) **reduced-fat
   coconut milk**
2 tablespoons chopped **mint
   leaves**
2 tablespoons chopped
   **coriander leaves**
**salt**

**Place** the liver in a small saucepan and add enough
water to cover. Add the peppercorns, season with salt
and poach over a low heat for about 10 minutes until
the liver is just firm but still pink inside. Don't overcook
it, or it will be tough. Remove from the heat and drain.
When cool enough to handle, cut the liver into small dice.

**Meanwhile,** heat the oil in a large frying pan over a
low heat. Add the chilli, onion, garlic and ginger, and fry
gently for 10–12 minutes until soft.

**Add** the remaining ingredients, including the diced
liver, and simmer gently, uncovered, over a low heat for
20 minutes or until the sauce is thick. Serve immediately
with naan bread and a salad.

**For curried pan-fried calf's liver**, season 4 thick
slices of calf's liver (about 200 g/7 oz each). Mix
2 tablespoons medium curry powder (see page 16) with
4 tablespoons plain flour and use to coat the liver. Heat
a large nonstick frying pan over a medium-high heat.
Spray the liver with cooking oil spray, add to the hot pan
and fry for 4–5 minutes on each side or until nicely
browned. Remove from the heat and serve immediately
with a crisp green salad and crusty bread.

# lamb rogan josh

Serves **4**

Preparation time **20 minutes**,
plus marinating

Cooking time **2 hours**

1 kg (2 lb) **lean lamb**, cubed

400 g (13 oz) can **chopped
tomatoes**

300 ml (½ pint) **water**

1 teaspoon **sugar**

2 tablespoons chopped
**coriander leaves**, plus extra
to garnish

**Marinade**

1 **onion**, roughly chopped

4 **garlic cloves**, roughly
chopped

2 teaspoons grated **fresh root
ginger**

1 large **fresh red chilli**,
chopped

2 teaspoons **ground coriander**

large pinch of **salt**

1 teaspoon **ground cumin**

1 teaspoon **ground turmeric**

½ teaspoon **ground
cinnamon**

½ teaspoon **ground white
pepper**

2 tablespoons **red wine
vinegar**

**Place** all the marinade ingredients in a food processor
and blend to a smooth paste. Place the lamb and
marinade in a non-metallic bowl and stir to coat evenly.
Cover and marinate in the refrigerator overnight.

**Place** the meat and marinade in a saucepan with the
tomatoes, measured water and sugar. Bring to the boil,
reduce the heat, cover and simmer gently for 1½ hours.

**Stir** in the coriander and cook, uncovered, for a further
25–30 minutes until the sauce is thick. Garnish with
coriander and serve with rice.

**For perfect rice**, to serve as an accompaniment, place
300 g (10 oz) basmati rice in a large saucepan with
1.5 litres (2½ pints) cold water and a large pinch of salt.
Bring to the boil, reduce the heat and simmer for
10 minutes. Drain the rice in a sieve then place the
sieve over the saucepan. Cover the whole sieve and pan
with a clean tea towel and leave to stand for 5 minutes.
Fluff up the grains with a fork and serve.

# beef, red pepper & squash curry

Serves **4**
Preparation time **15 minutes**
Cooking time **about 1¼ hours**

**cooking oil spray**
2 **onions**, finely chopped
750 g (1½ lb) **lean beef fillet**,
  cubed
2 **garlic cloves**, crushed
1 teaspoon peeled and grated
  **fresh root ginger**
1 dried **red Kashmiri chilli**
500 g (1 lb) **butternut
  squash**, peeled, deseeded
  and cubed
2 **red peppers**, cored,
  deseeded and cubed
4 tablespoons **medium curry
  powder** (see page 16)
1 litre (1¾ pints) **water**
**salt** and **pepper**
chopped **coriander leaves**,
  to garnish

**Spray** a large saucepan or casserole with cooking oil spray and place over a medium-high heat. Add the onion and cook gently for 12–15 minutes.

**Add** the meat, garlic, ginger, chilli, butternut squash, peppers and curry powder, and stir-fry slowly for a few minutes. Pour in the measured water and stir well.

**Bring** to the boil, cover tightly and reduce the heat to low. Simmer gently for 50–60 minutes until the meat and squash are tender. Season to taste, stir in the coriander and serve hot with rice.

**For lamb, potato & pumpkin curry,** substitute the beef for 750 g (1½ lb) cubed lean lamb and the butternut squash for 500 g (1 lb) peeled and cubed pumpkin. Replace the peppers with 3 medium potatoes, peeled and cubed, and cook as above. Serve with warmed parathas.

# bangkok sour pork curry

Serves **4**
Preparation time **20 minutes**
Cooking time **2¼ hours**

1 tablespoon **groundnut oil**
1 **onion**, finely chopped
1 teaspoon peeled and finely
  grated **galangal**
3 tablespoons **Thai red curry
  paste** (see page 17)
750 g (1½ lb) thick **pork
  steaks**, cubed
750 ml (1¼ pints) **chicken
  stock**
8 tablespoons finely chopped
  **fresh coriander root** and
  **stem**
2 **lemon grass stalks**, bruised
4 tablespoons **tamarind paste**
1 tablespoon **palm sugar** or
  **brown sugar**
6 **kaffir lime leaves**
small handful of **Thai basil
  leaves**, to garnish

**Preheat** the oven to 150°C (300°F), Gas Mark 2. Heat the oil in a large casserole and fry the onion over a medium heat for 3–4 minutes. Add the galangal, curry paste and pork and stir-fry for 4–5 minutes.

**Pour** in the stock and add the chopped coriander, lemon grass, tamarind, sugar and lime leaves. Bring to the boil, cover and cook in the preheated oven for 2 hours or until the pork is tender.

**Garnish** with Thai basil and serve the curry with steamed jasmine rice.

**For Bangkok sour pork curry with noodles**, cook 250 g (8 oz) thick egg noodles according to packet instructions. Fresh noodles, available in the chilled section of Oriental stores and large supermarkets, have the best texture, but dried noodles are a good substitute. Divide the noodles between 4 warmed bowls and ladle the curry, cooked as above, over the top. Sprinkle with chopped coriander leaves as well as the Thai basil.

# goat & vegetable curry

Serves **4**

Preparation time **10 minutes**, plus marinating

Cooking time **2–2¼ hours**

large pinch of **salt**

1 teaspoon **freshly ground black pepper**

1 tablespoon **medium curry powde**r (see page 16)

750 g (1½ lb) lean **goat** or **mutton**, cubed

1 tablespoon **groundnut oil**

2 **onions**, halved and thickly sliced

750 ml (1¼ pints) **lamb stock**

2 fresh **Scotch bonnet chillies**

2 **carrots**, chopped

4 **celery sticks**, roughly sliced

4 **potatoes**, peeled and cubed

6 tablespoons **coconut cream**

chopped **coriander leaves**, to garnish

**Sift** together the salt, pepper and curry powder, and rub into the cubes of meat. Set aside for 1 hour.

**Heat** the oil in a large saucepan over a medium-low heat. Add the meat and onion and cook, stirring, for 10–12 minutes until the meat is browned and well sealed.

**Add** the stock and chillies, reduce the heat to low, cover the pan and simmer for 1½ hours or until the meat is tender. Add the carrots, celery, potatoes and coconut cream, and continue cooking for a further 20–30 minutes or until the vegetables are tender and the gravy is thick.

**For Caribbean rice & beans**, to serve as an accompaniment, spray a saucepan with cooking oil spray. Add 4 sliced spring onions, 1 sliced garlic clove and ¼ finely chopped scotch bonnet chilli, and stir-fry over a gentle heat for 10–12 minutes until softened. Add 300 g (10 oz) long-grain rice and ½ teaspoon grated ginger, stir well and add 450 ml (¾ pint) vegetable stock, 200 ml (7 fl oz) reduced-fat coconut milk, 400 g (13 oz) can kidney beans, rinsed and drained, and 3 tablespoons thyme leaves. Bring to the boil and season to taste. Reduce the heat to low, cover the pan and cook gently for 10–12 minutes or until all the liquid has been absorbed. Remove from the heat and allow to stand, covered and undisturbed, for 10–15 minutes. Fluff up the grains with a fork and serve.

# slow-cooked beef curry

Serves **4–6**
Preparation time **20 minutes**
Cooking time **2¼ hours**

1 tablespoon **groundnut oil**
1 large **onion**, chopped
750 g (1 ½ lb) **stewing steak**, cubed
2 tablespoons **tomato purée**
3 **tomatoes**, chopped
250 ml (8 fl oz) **water**
3 tablespoons **fat-free natural yogurt**, plus extra to serve
1 teaspoon **nigella seeds**
**salt** and **pepper**

**Curry paste**
2 teaspoons **cumin seeds**
1 teaspoon **coriander seeds**
½ teaspoon **fennel seeds**
2 **garlic cloves**, chopped
1 tablespoon peeled and grated **fresh root ginger**
1–2 small **fresh green chillies**
1 teaspoon **paprika**
1 teaspoon **ground turmeric**
2 tablespoons **tomato purée**
2 tablespoons **groundnut oil**
25 g (1 oz) **coriander leaves**, plus extra to garnish

**Place** the whole spices for the curry paste in a small frying pan and dry-fry over a medium heat for 2–3 minutes until fragrant. Tip the contents of the pan into a mini blender and grind to a fine powder. Add the remaining curry paste ingredients and blend to a smooth paste.

**Heat** the oil in a large saucepan over a medium heat, add the onion and cook for 5–6 minutes or until beginning to colour, stirring occasionally. Add 3 tablespoons of the prepared curry paste and stir-fry for 1–2 minutes.

**Stir** in the beef and cook for 4–5 minutes or until the meat is browned and well coated. Stir in the tomato purée, tomatoes, measured water and yogurt, and bring to the boil. Reduce the heat, cover and simmer for 2 hours or until tender, adding more liquid if necessary.

**Season** to taste and ladle into warmed bowls. Sprinkle with the nigella seeds and garnish with coriander leaves. Serve hot with naan bread and yogurt.

### For slow-cooked lamb curry with spinach & chickpeas, make the curry as above, replacing the curry paste with 4 tablespoons ready-made Madras or rogan josh curry paste and the beef with 750 g (1 ½ lb) cubed lean leg of lamb. Stir a 400 g (13 oz) can chickpeas, rinsed and drained, into the curry with the yogurt. Cook as above, stirring in 125 g (4 oz) baby spinach at the end of the cooking time.

# stuffed aubergines with lamb

Serves **4**
Preparation time **20 minutes**
Cooking time **45 minutes**

2 large **aubergines**
1 tablespoon **groundnut oil**
1 **onion**, thinly sliced
1 teaspoon peeled and finely
    grated **fresh root ginger**
1 teaspoon **hot chilli powder**
1 tablespoon **medium curry
    paste**
2 **garlic cloves**, crushed
¼ teaspoon **ground turmeric**
1 teaspoon **ground coriander**
2 teaspoons **dried mint**
1 **ripe tomato**, finely chopped
500 g (1 lb) **lean minced
    lamb**
100 g (3½ oz) **roasted red
    peppers** in brine, drained
    and finely diced
2 tablespoons chopped
    **coriander leaves**
2 tablespoons chopped **mint
    leaves**
**salt**

**Preheat** the oven to 180°C (350°F), Gas Mark 4. Cut the aubergines in half lengthways, use a spoon to scoop out most of the flesh and discard it. Place the aubergines, cut sides up, on a baking sheet and set aside.

**Heat** the oil in a large frying pan over a medium heat. Add the onion and stir-fry for 4–5 minutes until soft. Now add the ginger, chilli powder, curry paste, garlic, turmeric, ground coriander, dried mint and chopped tomato, and stir-fry for 4–5 minutes. Season to taste.

**Add** the lamb and continue to stir-fry for 5–6 minutes over a high heat until well browned. Stir in the red pepper and herbs and mix well. Spoon the lamb mixture into the prepared aubergine shells and cook in the preheated oven for 20–25 minutes. Serve immediately with a herby tabbouleh.

**For minced lamb & aubergine curry**, heat 1 tablespoon groundnut oil in a nonstick wok or frying pan and add 1 finely chopped onion, 2 crushed garlic cloves, 2 teaspoons grated fresh root ginger and 2 sliced fresh red chillies, and stir-fry for 3–4 minutes. Cut 1 large aubergine into 1.5 cm (¾ inch) cubes, add to the pan and stir-fry for 2–3 minutes. Add 2 tablespoons medium curry powder (see page 16) and 625 g (1¼ lb) extra-lean minced lamb and stir-fry for 6–8 minutes over a high heat until sealed. Stir in a 400 g (13 oz) can chopped tomatoes and 1 teaspoon agave syrup and season to taste. Cook over a medium heat for 6–8 minutes or until the lamb is tender and cooked through. Remove from the heat, add a handful each of chopped coriander and mint leaves and serve with warm bread or rice.

# indonesian beef rendang

Serves **4–6**
Preparation time **30 minutes**
Cooking time **4½–5 hours**

2 tablespoons **groundnut oil**
750 g (1½ lb) **stewing steak**,
   sliced
750 ml (1¼ pints) **reduced-fat
   coconut milk**
1 tablespoon **palm sugar**
4 **kaffir lime leaves**, shredded
3 **star anise**
1 large **cinnamon stick**
½ teaspoon **salt**

**Spice paste**
large pinch of **salt**
1 teaspoon **ground turmeric**
½ teaspoon **chilli powder**
6 **garlic cloves**, chopped
5 cm (2 inch) piece of **fresh root
   ginger**, peeled and grated
5 cm (2 inch) piece of
   **galangal,** peeled and grated
1 teaspoon **black
   peppercorns**, crushed
4 **cardamom pods**
4 fresh **red chillies**, chopped
2 tablespoons chopped **lemon
   grass** (outer leaves removed)
3 large **onions**, chopped
1 tablespoon **tamarind paste**

**Place** the spice paste ingredients, up to and including the chillies, in a food processor until roughly chopped, or pound using a mortar and pestle. Add the lemon grass and onion, and process or pound to a dry paste. Add the tamarind paste and blend to mix.

**Heat** the oil in a large saucepan over a medium-high heat. Working in batches, fry the beef for a few minutes until browned on all sides. Remove each batch with a slotted spoon and set aside. Add the spice paste to the hot pan and fry for 2–3 minutes, stirring constantly. Return the beef to the pan with all the remaining ingredients. Pour in 250 ml (8 fl oz) water, reduce the heat and bring slowly to the boil, stirring constantly.

**Reduce** the heat again to as low as possible and simmer very gently for 4–4½ hours, stirring occasionally, until the meat is tender and the sauce has reduced and thickened. Increase the heat and, stirring constantly, fry the beef in the thick sauce until it is a rich brown colour and nearly all of the sauce has been absorbed. Serve hot.

**For egg rendang**, omit the beef and fry 1 roughly chopped onion and 2 potatoes, cut into large dice, for 5 minutes instead. Add the spice paste and remaining ingredients. Simmer for 1 hour, then remove the potatoes and set aside. Continue cooking until the sauce has reduced and thickened. Return the potatoes to the pan with 6 hard-boiled eggs, peeled and halved, and cook for 5 minutes to heat through.

# curried oxtail & chickpea stew

Serves **4**
Preparation time **20 minutes**
Cooking time **about 3 hours**

1.5 kg (3 lb) **oxtail,** cubed
1 tablespoon **groundnut oil**
2 teaspoons **ground allspice**
2 teaspoons **medium curry powder** (see page 18)
1.5 litres (2½ pints) **beef stock**
4 **carrots,** cut into chunks
2 **onions,** finely chopped
3 **garlic cloves,** finely chopped
2 **thyme** sprigs
1 fresh **Scotch bonnet chilli**
400 g (14 oz) can **chopped tomatoes**
4 tablespoons **cornflour**
400 g (14 oz) can **chickpeas,** rinsed and drained
**salt** and **pepper**

**Bring** a large saucepan of water to the boil. Add the oxtail and bring back to the boil. Reduce the heat and simmer for 10–12 minutes. Drain and pat dry with kitchen paper. Season to taste.

**Heat** the oil in a large saucepan or casserole and brown the oxtail on both sides for 6–8 minutes. Add the allspice, curry powder, beef stock, carrots, onion, garlic, thyme, chilli, tomatoes and cornflour. Stir to mix well and bring to the boil. Cover and simmer gently for 2½ hours or until the oxtail is meltingly tender.

**Add** the chickpeas and cook for a further 15 minutes. Serve the stew immediately with mashed potatoes or crusty bread.

### For curried lamb shanks with chickpeas, heat

1 tablespoon groundnut oil in a wide casserole and brown 4 lamb shanks on all sides for 6–8 minutes. Add 2 teaspoons ground allspice, 2 tablespoons medium curry powder, 750 ml (1¼ pints) lamb stock, a 400 g (13 oz) can chopped tomatoes, 1 finely chopped carrot, 1 finely chopped onion, 4 chopped garlic cloves, 1 thyme sprig and 1 scotch bonnet chilli. Season and bring to the boil. Cover and simmer gently for 2½ hours or until the meat is falling off the bone. Serve with rice or bread.

# thai jungle curry with beef

Serves **4**

Preparation time **10 minutes**

Cooking time **about 25 minutes**

1 tablespoon **groundnut oil**

2–3 tablespoons **Thai red curry paste** (see page 17)

1 teaspoon **ground turmeric**

¼ teaspoon **ground allspice**

500 g (1 lb) **lean beef**, thinly sliced

400 ml (14 fl oz) **reduced-fat coconut milk**

250 ml (8 fl oz) **beef stock**

3 tablespoons **Thai fish sauce**

50 g (2 oz) **palm sugar** or **brown sugar**

4–5 tablespoons **tamarind paste**

**salt** and **pepper**

**To garnish**

½ **red pepper,** cut into thin strips

2 **spring onions**, shredded

**Heat** the oil in a saucepan and stir-fry the curry paste, turmeric and allspice over a medium heat for 3–4 minutes or until fragrant.

**Add** the beef and stir-fry for 4–5 minutes. Add the coconut milk, stock, fish sauce, sugar and tamarind. Reduce the heat and simmer for 10–15 minutes or until the beef is tender. Season to taste and add a little stock or water if the sauce is too dry.

**Spoon** into serving bowls, garnish with strips of red pepper and spring onion and serve with rice.

**For Thai jungle curry with pork**, replace the beef with 750 g (1½ lb) pork belly, cut into 2.5 cm (1 inch) pieces. Add to the saucepan after the curry paste is fragrant and cook for 4–5 minutes. Add the coconut milk, 500 ml (17 fl oz) vegetable stock, 20 whole small shallots, 50 g (2 oz) roasted peanuts, 1 tablespoon shredded ginger, the fish sauce, sugar and tamarind paste and simmer for 45 minutes–1 hour, or until the pork is tender. Cook this a day ahead so you can discard any fat that rises to the top on cooling. Reheat it when ready to serve, spoon into serving bowls and garnish with a few slices of red chilli.

# nonya meatball curry

Serves **4**
Preparation time **25 minutes,**
  plus chilling
Cooking time **30 minutes**

3 teaspoons crushed **garlic**
100 g (3½ oz) **shallots**, finely
  chopped
1 teaspoon grated **galangal** or
  fresh **root ginger**
6 long **red chillies**, plus extra
  for garnish
6 tablespoons **sunflower oil**
400 g (13 oz) canned
  **chopped tomatoes**
1 tablespoon **kecap asin**
400 ml (14 fl oz) **coconut milk**
**salt** and **pepper**
chopped fresh **coriander**,
  to garnish

**Meatballs**
2 **eggs**
2 teaspoons **cornflour**
2 **garlic cloves**, crushed
2 tablespoons finely chopped
  fresh **coriander**
2 **red chillies**, finely chopped
750 g (1½ lb) **minced beef**

**Make** the meatballs by combining all the ingredients together in a large mixing bowl. Season well and roll tablespoons of the mixture into walnut-sized balls. Place on a tray, cover and chill for 3–4 hours or overnight if time permits.

**Place** the garlic, shallots, galangal or ginger, chillies and half the oil in a small food processor and blend to a paste.

**Heat** the remaining oil in a large nonstick wok, add the paste and stir-fry for 1–2 minutes. Add the tomatoes, kecap asin and coconut milk and bring to the boil. Reduce the heat to low and simmer gently for 10 minutes.

**Add** the meatballs to the curry and simmer for 12–15 minutes, stirring occasionally. Remove from the heat and serve with rice noodles or steamed rice, as preferred. Garnish with sliced red chillies and chopped coriander.

**For pork meatball curry**, replace the minced beef with the same quantity of minced pork, and instead of kecap asin substitute 1 tablespoon dark soy sauce and 1 teaspoon Thai fish sauce. Cook as above.

poultry
& eggs

# balti chicken

Serves **4**
Preparation time **15 minutes**
Cooking time **20–25 minutes**

1 tablespoon **groundnut oil**
2 **onions**, thinly sliced
2 **fresh red chillies**, deseeded
 and thinly sliced
6–8 **curry leaves**
200 ml (7 fl oz) **water**
3 **garlic cloves**, crushed
1 teaspoon peeled and finely
 grated **fresh root ginger**
1 tablespoon **ground
 coriander**
2 tablespoons **Madras curry
 powder**
500 g (1 lb) **minced chicken**
400 g (13 oz) fresh or frozen
 **peas**
4 tablespoons **lemon juice**
small handful of chopped
 **mint leaves**
small handful of chopped
 **coriander leaves**
**salt**

**Heat** the oil in a large wok or frying pan over a medium heat. Add the onion, chilli and curry leaves, and stir-fry for 4–5 minutes. Add 4 tablespoons of the measured water and continue to stir-fry for a further 2–3 minutes.

**Add** the garlic, ginger, ground coriander, curry powder and chicken, and stir-fry over a high heat for 10 minutes. Add the remaining measured water and the peas, and continue to cook for 6–8 minutes until the chicken is cooked through.

**Remove** from the heat and stir in the lemon juice and herbs. Season to taste, and serve immediately with warmed chapatis and natural yogurt.

**For creamy chicken & vegetable curry**, heat 1 tablespoon groundnut oil in a large wok or frying pan. Add 1 chopped onion, 1 sliced red chilli, 6 curry leaves, 2 teaspoons each of crushed fresh root ginger and garlic, and 2 tablespoons mild curry powder (see page 16). Stir-fry for 1–2 minutes, then add 625 g (1¼ lb) diced skinless chicken breast fillets. Stir-fry for 3–4 minutes, then add 500 ml (17 fl oz) chicken stock and 200 ml (7 fl oz) reduced-fat coconut milk. Bring to the boil and cook for 12–15 minutes or until the chicken is cooked through. Stir in 200 g (7 oz) frozen peas and cook over a high heat for 4–5 minutes. Season and serve with rice.

# chicken kofta curry

Serves **4**
Preparation time **15 minutes**
Cooking time **25 minutes**

750 g (1½ lb) **minced chicken**
2 teaspoons peeled and finely grated **fresh root ginger**
2 **garlic cloves**, crushed
2 teaspoons **fennel seeds**, crushed
1 teaspoon **ground cinnamon**
1 teaspoon **chilli powder**
**cooking oil spray**
500 ml (17 fl oz) **tomato passata with onions and garlic**
1 teaspoon **ground turmeric**
2 tablespoons **medium curry powder** (see page 16)
1 teaspoon **agave syrup**
**salt** and **pepper**

**To serve**
100 ml (3½ fl oz) **fat-free natural yogurt,** whisked
pinch of **chilli powder**
chopped **mint leaves**

**Place** the mince in a bowl with the ginger, garlic, fennel seeds, cinnamon and chilli powder. Season to taste and mix thoroughly with your hands until well combined. Form the mixture into walnut-sized balls.

**Spray** a large nonstick frying pan with cooking oil spray and place over a medium heat. Add the chicken balls and stir-fry for 4–5 minutes or until lightly browned. Transfer to a plate and keep warm.

**Pour** the passata into the frying pan and add the turmeric, curry powder and agave syrup. Bring to the boil, then reduce the heat to a simmer, season to taste and carefully place the chicken balls in the sauce. Cover and cook gently for 15–20 minutes, turning the balls occasionally, until they are cooked through.

**Serve** immediately, drizzled with the yogurt and sprinkled with chilli powder and mint leaves.

**For quick chunky chicken Madras**, replace the minced chicken with cubed, skinless chicken breast fillets and the medium curry powder with Madras curry powder (see page 84). Cook as above and add 300 g (10 oz) peas for the last 5 minutes of cooking. Serve hot.

# tandoori chicken skewers

Serves **4**

Preparation time **10 minutes**, plus marinating

Cooking time **about 10 minutes**

200 ml (7 fl oz) **fat-free natural yogurt**

3 tablespoons **tandoori powder**

1 tablespoon finely grated **garlic**

1 tablespoon peeled and finely grated **fresh root ginger**

juice of 2 **limes**

1 kg (2 lb) skinless **chicken breast fillets**, cubed

2 **yellow peppers**, cored, deseeded and cubed

2 **red peppers**, cored, deseeded and cubed

**salt** and **pepper**

**Place** the yogurt, tandoori powder, garlic, ginger and lime juice in a large non-metallic bowl. Mix well, season to taste and add the chicken. Toss to coat evenly, cover and marinate in the refrigerator for 6–8 hours or overnight.

**Preheat** the grill to medium-hot. Thread the chicken on to 12 metal skewers, alternating with the pepper pieces, and grill for 4–5 minutes on each side until the edges are lightly charred and the chicken is cooked through. Serve with warmed naan breads and chutney or pomegranate raita.

**For pomegranate raita**, to serve as an accompaniment, place 375 ml (13 fl oz) fat-free natural yogurt in a bowl. Coarsely grate ½ cucumber, squeeze out the excess liquid and add to the yogurt with a small handful of finely chopped mint leaves, 2 teaspoons lightly dry-roasted cumin seeds and 100 g (3½ oz) pomegranate seeds. Season, mix well and chill until ready to serve.

# sri lankan tomato & egg curry

Serves **4**
Preparation time **10 minutes**
Cooking time **15–20 minutes**

1 tablespoon **groundnut oil**
1 **onion**, finely chopped
10 **curry leaves**
3 **garlic cloves**, finely
  chopped
2 teaspoons peeled and finely
  grated **fresh root ginger**
2 **fresh green chillies**, finely
  chopped
3 tablespoons **medium curry
  powder** (see page 16)
400 g (13 oz) can **chopped
  tomatoes**
8–12 **eggs**, hard-boiled and
  peeled
6 tablespoons finely chopped
  **coriander leaves**
salt

**Heat** the oil in a large nonstick frying pan and add the onion, curry leaves, garlic, ginger and chillies. Stir-fry over a medium heat for 6–8 minutes.

**Sprinkle** over the curry powder and stir-fry for 1–2 minutes until fragrant. Stir in the chopped tomatoes, season to taste and stir to mix well.

**Add** the eggs and bring to the boil. Reduce the heat and simmer gently for 4–5 minutes. Remove from the heat and stir in the coriander. Halve the eggs and serve immediately with rice.

**For Sri Lankan coconut relish**, to serve as an accompaniment, mix 1 tablespoon grated red onion with 1 crushed garlic clove, 50 g (2 oz) grated fresh coconut, 1 teaspoon chilli powder, 1 teaspoon paprika, 1 tablespoon anchovy sauce and the juice of 2 limes. Leave to stand at room temperature for 30 minutes before serving with the curry and rice.

# bhoona chicken curry

Serves **4**
Preparation time **10 minutes**,
  plus marinating
Cooking time **8–10 minutes**

125 ml (4 fl oz) **fat-free
  natural yogurt**
juice of 2 **limes**
2 **garlic cloves**, finely chopped
1 teaspoon **ground turmeric**
1 tablespoon **mild chilli
  powder**
1 teaspoon **cardamom seeds**,
  crushed
large pinch of **sea salt**
1 tablespoon **ground
  coriander**
1 tablespoon **ground cumin**
4 skinless **chicken breast
  fillets**, cut into strips
1 tablespoon **groundnut oil**
1 teaspoon **garam masala**
handful of roughly chopped
  **coriander leaves**

**Place** the yogurt, lime juice, garlic, turmeric, chilli powder, cardamom, salt, ground coriander and cumin in a large non-metallic bowl. Mix well and add the chicken. Toss to coat evenly, cover and marinate in the refrigerator for 6–8 hours or overnight.

**Heat** the oil in a large nonstick frying pan over a medium-high heat, and stir-fry the chicken mixture for 8–10 minutes until tender and cooked through.

**Sprinkle** over the garam masala and chopped coriander, stir well and serve with steamed rice.

**For masala chicken kebabs**, prepare the marinade as above and add 4 skinless chicken breast fillets, cut into cubes. Marinate in the refrigerator for 6–8 hours or overnight if time permits. When ready to cook, thread the chicken pieces on to 8 metal skewers and cook under a medium-hot grill for 5–6 minutes on each side or until cooked through. Serve with warmed naan bread or rice.

# souffléd curried omelette

Serves **4**
Preparation time **25 minutes**
Cooking time **about 20 minutes**

1 tablespoon **groundnut oil**
4 **garlic cloves**, crushed
8 **spring onions**, finely sliced
1 **red chilli**, finely sliced
1 tablespoon **medium curry powder** (see page 16)
4 **tomatoes**, peeled, deseeded and finely chopped
small handful of finely chopped **coriander leaves**
small handful of finely chopped **mint leaves**,
8 large **eggs**, separated
**salt** and **pepper**

**Heat** half the oil in an ovenproof frying pan over a medium heat. Add the garlic, spring onions and red chilli and stir-fry for 1–2 minutes. Stir in the curry powder, tomatoes and chopped herbs and stir-fry for 20–30 seconds. Remove from the heat, season to taste and allow to cool slightly.

**Place** the egg whites in a large bowl and whisk until soft peaks form. Gently beat the egg yolks in a separate bowl, then fold into the egg whites with the tomato mixture until well combined.

**Wipe** out the pan with kitchen paper and place over a medium heat. Add the remaining oil and, when hot, pour in the egg mixture. Reduce the heat and cook gently for 8–10 minutes or until the base is starting to set. Transfer the pan to a preheated medium-hot grill and cook for 4–5 minutes or until the top is puffed, lightly golden and almost set. Serve immediately with toast and a crisp green salad.

**For Indian spicy scrambled eggs**, heat 1 tablespoon groundnut oil in a large nonstick frying pan over a gentle heat. Beat 8 eggs in a bowl and add 1 finely chopped red onion, 2 sliced green chillies, 1 finely chopped tomato, 1 teaspoon grated peeled ginger and a small handful of finely chopped coriander leaves. Season, pour into the pan and cook, stirring occasionally, for 5–6 minutes or until lightly scrambled. Serve immediately with toast.

# thai jungle curry with duck

Serves **4**
Preparation time **20 minutes**
Cooking time **30 minutes**

2 tablespoons **Thai green
    curry paste** (see page 17)
2 tablespoons finely chopped
    **lemon grass** (tough outer
    leaves removed)
3 **kaffir lime leaves**, finely
    shredded
1 teaspoon **shrimp paste**
6 **garlic cloves**, crushed
5 **shallots**, finely chopped
3 tablespoons finely chopped
    **coriander root**
2 tablespoons **groundnut oil**
**cooking oil spray**
625 g (1¼ lb) skinless **duck
    breast fillets**, thinly sliced
400 ml (14 fl oz) **chicken
    stock**
1 tablespoon **Thai fish sauce**
65 g (2½ oz) **canned
    bamboo shoots**, rinsed and
    drained
4 baby **aubergines**, quartered
small handful of **Thai basil
    leaves**

**Place** the green curry paste, lemon grass, lime leaves, shrimp paste, garlic, shallots, coriander root and groundnut oil in a mini blender and blend to a smooth paste, adding a little water if necessary.

**Spray** a large nonstick wok with cooking oil spray, place over a high heat and add the curry paste. Stir-fry for 1–2 minutes, then add the duck. Stir-fry for 4–5 minutes until sealed, then pour in the stock and fish sauce and bring to the boil. Remove the duck from the pan with a slotted spoon, set aside and keep warm.

**Add** the bamboo shoots and aubergines to the pan and cook for 12–15 minutes or until tender.

**Return** the meat to the pan and cook gently for 3–4 minutes. Stir in half the basil leaves and remove from the heat. Ladle into bowls, garnish with the remaining basil and serve with jasmine rice.

**For jungle curry with pigeon**, replace the duck with 8 pigeon breasts, thinly sliced. Follow the recipe above, using light soy sauce instead of Thai fish sauce, and replacing the bamboo shoots with canned water chestnuts for a crunchy texture. Cook as above until the pigeon is tender.

# indonesian yellow drumstick curry

Serves **4**
Preparation time **15 minutes**
Cooking time **40–45 minutes**

2 **fresh red chillies,** roughly
    chopped, plus extra to garnish
2 **shallots,** roughly chopped
3 **garlic cloves,** chopped
4 tablespoons finely chopped
    **lemon grass** (tough outer
    leaves removed)
1 tablespoon peeled and finely
    chopped **galangal**
2 teaspoons **ground turmeric**
1 teaspoon **cayenne pepper**
1 teaspoon **ground coriander**
1 teaspoon **ground cumin**
¼ teaspoon **ground cinnamon**
3 tablespoons **Thai fish sauce**
1 tablespoon **palm sugar** or
    **brown sugar**
4 **kaffir lime leaves,** finely
    shredded
400 ml (14 fl oz) **reduced-fat**
    **coconut milk**
juice of ½ **lime**
12 large **chicken drumsticks,**
    skinned
200 g (7 oz) baby **new**
    **potatoes,** peeled
10–12 **Thai basil leaves,**
    to garnish

**Preheat** the oven to 190°C (375°F), Gas Mark 5.
Place the chillies, shallots, garlic, lemon grass, galangal,
turmeric, cayenne, coriander, cumin, cinnamon, fish
sauce, sugar, lime leaves, coconut milk and lime juice in
a food processor, and blend until fairly smooth.

**Arrange** the chicken drumsticks in a single layer in an
ovenproof casserole. Scatter over the potatoes. Pour
over the spice paste to coat the chicken and potatoes
evenly. Cover and cook in the preheated oven for
40–45 minutes until the chicken is cooked through and
the potatoes are tender. Serve hot, garnished with basil
and chopped red chilli.

**For tandoori drumstick curry**, arrange 12 large,
skinned chicken drumsticks in a single layer in an
ovenproof casserole. Mix 300 ml (½ pint) fat-free
natural yogurt with 4 tablespoons tandoori paste and
the juice of 2 lemons. Season and pour this mixture
over the chicken to coat evenly. Cover and cook in
a preheated oven at 180°C (350°), Gas Mark 4, for
35–40 minutes, then uncover and continue to cook for
10–15 minutes or until cooked through. Serve warm
with a crisp green salad.

# creamy fragrant chicken curry

Serves **4**
Preparation time **15 minutes**
Cooking time **30–35 minutes**

1 tablespoon **groundnut oil**
2 **bay leaves**
1 **cinnamon stick**
1 teaspoon **ground cardamom**
4 **cloves**
2 teaspoons **cumin seeds**
1 large **onion**, finely chopped
2 tablespoons finely grated **garlic**
2 tablespoons peeled and finely grated **fresh root ginger**
1 tablespoon **ground coriander**
1 tablespoon **ground cumin**
200 g (7 oz) canned **chopped tomatoes**
750 g (1½ lb) skinless, boneless **chicken thighs**, cubed
1 teaspoon **chilli powder**
250 ml (8 fl oz) **water**
125 ml (4 fl oz) **fat-free natural yogurt**, whisked
small handful chopped **coriander leaves**
**salt**

**Heat** the oil in a large frying pan over a high heat. When hot, add the bay leaves, cinnamon, cardamom, cloves and cumin seeds. Stir-fry for 30 seconds until fragrant, then add the onion. Stir-fry for 4–5 minutes until the onion is soft.

**Add** the garlic, ginger, ground coriander and cumin, and fry for 1 minute. Add the tomatoes and continue stir-frying for another minute.

**Add** the chicken, chilli powder and measured water. Season to taste and bring to the boil. Cover the pan, reduce the heat to medium-low and simmer gently for 25 minutes, turning the chicken pieces now and then. Remove the pan from the heat and stir in the yogurt and coriander. Serve with steamed white rice.

### For quick minced chicken & coconut curry, heat
1 tablespoon groundnut oil in a large frying pan or wok. Add 625 g (1¼ lb) minced chicken and 2 tablespoons mild curry paste and stir-fry for 3–4 minutes over a high heat until the chicken is sealed and cooked through. Add 400 ml (14 fl oz) reduced-fat coconut milk and stir and cook over a high heat for 3–4 minutes. Season, remove from the heat and serve with jasmine rice or crusty bread.

# chicken, okra & red lentil dhal

Serves **4**
Preparation time **15 minutes**
Cooking time **45 minutes**

2 teaspoons **ground cumin**
1 teaspoon **ground coriander**
½ teaspoon **cayenne pepper**
¼ teaspoon **ground turmeric**
500 g (1 lb) skinless, boneless
   **chicken thighs**, cut into
   large pieces
2 tablespoons **groundnut oil**
1 **onion**, sliced
2 **garlic cloves**, crushed
25 g (1 oz) **fresh root ginger**,
   peeled and finely chopped
750 ml (1¼ pints) **water**
300 g (10 oz) **red lentils**,
   rinsed
200 g (7 oz) **okra**
small handful of **coriander**
   leaves, chopped
**salt**
**lime wedges**, to garnish

**Mix** the cumin, coriander, cayenne and turmeric and toss with the chicken pieces.

**Heat** the oil in a large saucepan. Fry the chicken pieces in batches until deep golden, transferring each batch to a plate. Add the onion to the pan and fry for 5 minutes until golden. Stir in the garlic and ginger and cook for a further 1 minute.

**Return** the chicken to the pan and add the measured water. Bring to the boil, reduce the heat and simmer very gently, covered, for 20 minutes until the chicken is cooked through. Add the lentils and cook for 5 minutes.

**Stir** in the okra, coriander and a little salt and cook for a further 5 minutes until the lentils are tender but not completely pulpy. Serve in shallow bowls with lime wedges, chutney and poppadums.

**For chicken, courgette & chilli dhal**, follow the main recipe but replace the okra with 3 medium courgettes, thinly sliced. For a hotter flavour, add 1 thinly sliced medium-strength red chilli with the garlic and ginger.

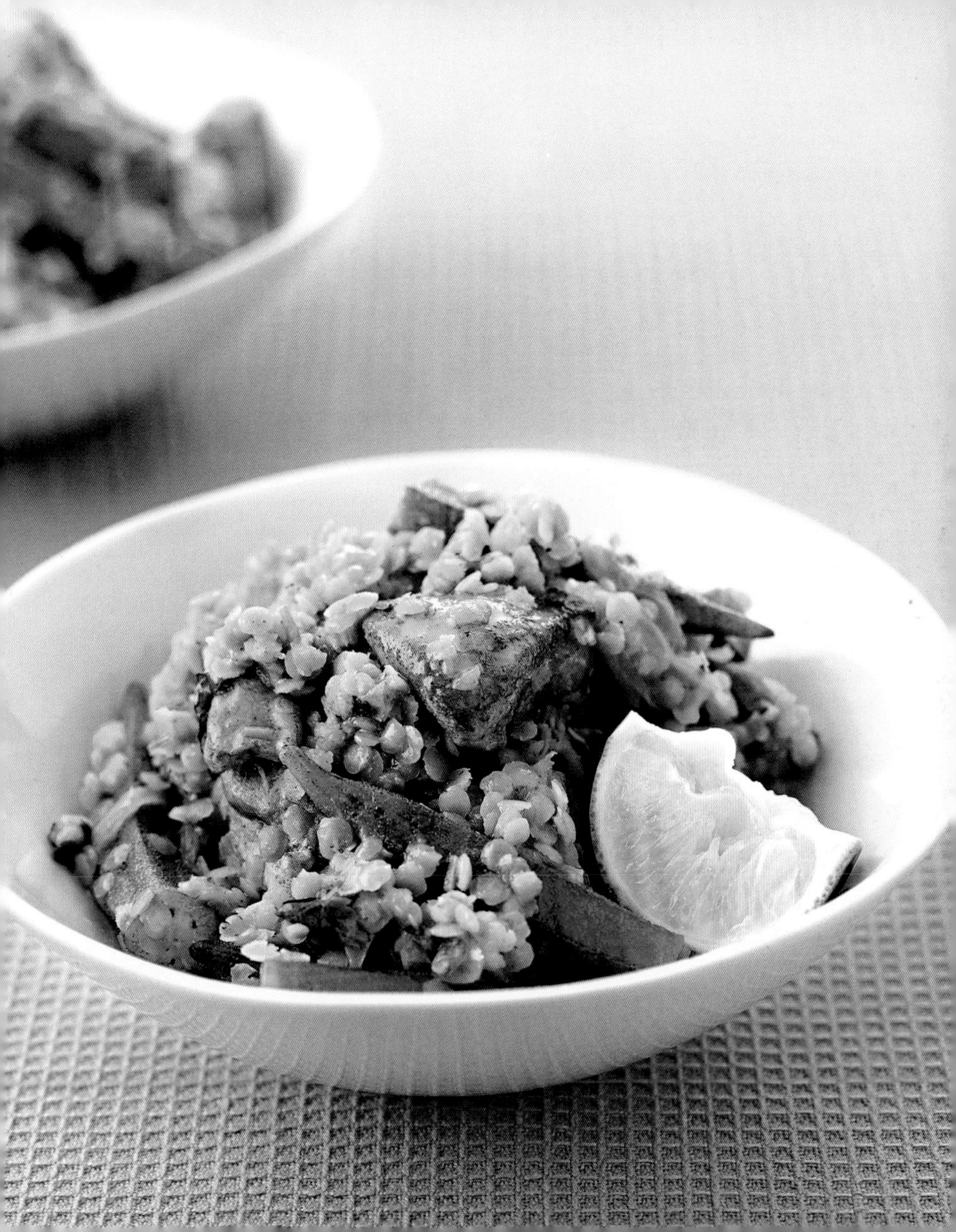

# goan xacutti duck

Serves **4**

Preparation time **20 minutes**, plus marinating

Cooking time **40–50 minutes**

750 g (1 ½ lb) skinless **duck breast fillets**, cubed

2 tablespoons **desiccated coconut**

1 tablespoon **groundnut oil**

2 large **onions**, finely chopped

1 tablespoon **tomato purée**

4 fresh **red chillies**

1 teaspoon **ground cloves**

2 tablespoons **garam masala**

1 **cinnamon stick**

500 ml (17 fl oz) **water**

chopped **coriander leaves**, to garnish

**lime wedges**, to serve

**Xacutti marinade**

1 tablespoon **garlic purée**

1 tablespoon **ginger purée**

2 tablespoons finely chopped **coriander leaves**

1 tablespoon **tamarind paste**

1 teaspoon **ground turmeric**

1 teaspoon **chilli powder**

**Mix** all the marinade ingredients together in a large bowl. Add the duck and toss to coat well. Cover and marinate in the refrigerator for 6–8 hours or overnight.

**Heat** a small frying pan over a low heat and dry-roast the coconut for a few minutes until lightly golden. Remove from the heat and set aside.

**Heat** the oil in a large saucepan over a medium heat and fry the onion for 8–10 minutes until soft and lightly browned. Add the roasted coconut, tomato purée, chillies, cloves, garam masala and cinnamon stick. Stir well to blend. Add the duck with the marinade and stir-fry over a high heat for 5 minutes.

**Add** the measured water and bring to the boil. Reduce the heat to low and simmer, covered, for 25–30 minutes until the duck is tender and the sauce is thick. Garnish with chopped coriander and serve with lime wedges for squeezing.

**For chicken xacutti skewers**, mix all the marinade ingredients in a non-metallic bowl with 200 ml (7 fl oz) fat-free natural yogurt. Add 750 g (1 ½ lb) skinless, boneless chicken thighs, season to taste, toss to mix well and marinate in the refrigerator for 6–8 hours. Thread the chicken on to 8 metal skewers and cook under a medium-hot grill for 5–6 minutes on each side or until cooked through. Serve immediately, garnished with chopped coriander.

# phillipino chicken curry

Serves **4**

Preparation time **10 minutes**, plus marinating

Cooking time **40–50 minutes**

750 g (1½ lb) skinless, boneless **chicken thighs**

2 tablespoons **medium curry powder** (see page 16)

1 tablespoon **groundnut oil**

4 **garlic cloves**, crushed

1 **onion**, sliced

4 small **tomatoes**, chopped

400 ml (14 fl oz) **reduced-fat coconut milk**

250 ml (8 fl oz) **chicken stock**

3 **potatoes**, peeled and quartered

**salt**

**Place** the chicken in a non-metallic bowl and sprinkle over the curry powder. Toss to mix well and marinate in the refrigerator for 30 minutes.

**Heat** the oil in a large saucepan over a medium-high heat. Add the garlic, onion and tomatoes, and fry for 3–4 minutes. Add the marinated chicken and stir-fry for 4–5 minutes.

**Add** the coconut milk, stock and potatoes and season to taste. Bring to the boil, reduce the heat to medium-low and simmer gently for 30–40 minutes until the chicken is tender. Serve hot with rice and pickles.

**For Phillipino chicken skewers**, cut 750 g (1½ lb) skinless, boneless chicken thighs into bite-sized pieces and place in a bowl with 100 ml (3½ fl oz) reduced-fat coconut milk, 6 tablespoons tomato purée, 4 crushed garlic cloves and 2 tablespoons medium curry powder (see page 18). Season, toss to mix well and marinate for 6–8 hours in the refrigerator. Thread the chicken on to 8 metal skewers and cook under a medium-hot grill for 5–6 minutes on each side or until cooked through. Serve with lime wedges.

# spinach & chicken curry

Serves **4**

Preparation time **15 minutes,**
plus marinating

Cooking time **about 1 hour**

5 tablespoons **fat-free natural yogurt**

2 tablespoons finely grated **garlic**

2 tablespoons peeled and finely grated **fresh root ginger**

1 tablespoon **ground coriander**

1 tablespoon **medium curry powder** (see page 16)

750 g (1½ lb) skinless **chicken breast fillets,** cubed

400 g (13 oz) **frozen spinach**

1 tablespoon **groundnut oil**

1 **onion,** finely chopped

2 teaspoons **cumin seeds**

400 ml (14 fl oz) **chicken stock**

1 tablespoon **lemon juice**

**salt** and **pepper**

**Mix** the yogurt, garlic, ginger, coriander and curry powder in a large non-metallic bowl. Season to taste and add the chicken. Toss to mix well, cover and marinate in the refrigerator for 8–10 hours.

**Place** the frozen spinach in a saucepan and cook over a medium heat for 6–8 minutes until defrosted. Season to taste and drain thoroughly. Transfer to a food processor and blend until smooth.

**Heat** the oil in a large nonstick frying pan with a lid over a low heat. Add the onion and fry gently for 10–12 minutes until soft and translucent. Add the cumin seeds and stir-fry for 1 minute until fragrant. Increase the heat to high, and add the chicken mixture. Stir-fry for 6–8 minutes.

**Pour** in the stock and spinach purée and bring to the boil. Reduce the heat, cover and simmer gently for 25–30 minutes until the chicken is cooked through. Uncover the pan, season to taste and cook over a high heat for 3–4 minutes, stirring often. Remove from the heat and stir in the lemon juice. Serve immediately.

**For duck curry with spinach**, cut 4 skinless duck breast fillets into chunks. Heat 1 tablespoon groundnut oil in a large saucepan over a medium-low heat and stir-fry 1 chopped onion for 8–10 minutes until tender, then add 2 tablespoons each of grated garlic and ginger. Increase the heat, add the duck and stir-fry for 2–3 minutes. Stir in 1 tablespoon medium curry powder (see page 18) and cook for 1 minute. Add 400 ml (14 fl oz) chicken stock and bring to the boil. Reduce the heat, cover and simmer for 25–30 minutes. Stir in 150 g (5 oz) baby spinach and cook for 3–4 minutes or until just wilted.

# chicken mussaman curry

Serves **4**
Preparation time **10 minutes**
Cooking time **35–40 minutes**

1 tablespoon **groundnut oil**
1 large **onion**, sliced
4 tablespoons **mussaman
   curry paste**
400 ml (14 fl oz) **reduced-fat
   coconut milk**
750 g (1½ lb) skinless
   **chicken breast fillets,**
   cubed
2 tablespoons **Thai fish sauce**
2 tablespoons **lime juice**
1 teaspoon **agave syrup**
100 g (3½ oz) **baby
   aubergines,** thinly sliced
2 tablespoons chopped **Thai
   basil leaves**

**Heat** the oil in a wok or frying pan over a medium heat.
Add the onion and fry for 6–8 minutes until soft.

**Blend** the curry paste with a little of the coconut milk
and add to the pan. Fry for 1 minute, then add the
chicken and stir vigorously for 3 minutes. Add the
remaining coconut milk, fish sauce, lime juice and agave
syrup. Stir well, reduce the heat to low and simmer
gently for 20 minutes.

**Increase** the heat to high, add the aubergines and
cook for 6–8 minutes. Remove from the heat, stir in the
chopped basil and serve immediately.

**For homemade mussaman curry paste**, place
100 g (3½ oz) unsalted peanuts in a mini blender
with 2 sliced shallots, 2 teaspoons dried red chillies,
2 teaspoons grated galangal or ginger, 2 tablespoons
chopped lemon grass, 2 teaspoons each of coriander
seeds and cumin seeds, ¼ teaspoon ground nutmeg,
1 teaspoon ground cinnamon, a pinch of ground cloves,
1 teaspoon ground cardamom, 2 tablespoons Thai fish
sauce, 1 teaspoon shrimp paste and 2 teaspoons palm
sugar. Add 8–10 tablespoons reduced-fat coconut milk
and blend until fairly smooth. Store any leftover paste
in an airtight jar in the refrigerator for up to 1 week, or
freeze in small portions for later use.

# vegetables

# potato & french bean curry

Serves **4**

Preparation time **20 minutes**

Cooking time **6–8 minutes**

1 tablespoon **groundnut oil**

4 teaspoons **cumin seeds**

1 teaspoon **medium curry powder** (see page 16)

1 **fresh green chilli,** finely sliced

2 teaspoons **ground cumin**

2 teaspoons **ground coriander**

1 teaspoon **ground turmeric**

4 **plum tomatoes,** peeled, deseeded and finely diced

500 g (1 lb) baby **new potatoes,** halved and boiled

400 g (13 oz) **French beans,** cut into 1 cm (½ inch) lengths and blanched

6 tablespoons chopped **mint leaves**

juice of 1 large **lime**

**salt** and **pepper**

**Heat** the oil in a large nonstick wok or frying pan over a medium-high heat. Add the cumin seeds, curry powder and green chilli and stir-fry for 1–2 minutes until fragrant.

**Add** the ground spices, tomatoes, potatoes and green beans. Season to taste and stir-fry briskly over a high heat for 4–5 minutes. Remove from the heat and stir in the mint. Squeeze over the lime juice and serve immediately.

**For simple pilau rice**, to serve as an accompaniment, place 1 tablespoon mild curry powder (see page 18) in a medium saucepan with 4 crushed green cardamom pods, 1 cinnamon stick, 2 cloves and 300 g (10 oz) basmati rice. Add 650 ml (1 pint 2 fl oz) boiling water, season and bring to the boil. Reduce the heat to low, cover the pan and cook gently for 10–12 minutes or until all the liquid has been absorbed. Remove from the heat and allow to stand, covered and undisturbed, for 10–15 minutes. Fluff up the grains with a fork and serve.

# curried cabbage & carrot stir-fry

Serves **4**
Preparation time **10 minutes**
Cooking time **about 15 minutes**

1 tablespoon **groundnut oil**
4 **shallots**, finely chopped
2 teaspoons peeled and finely grated **fresh root ginger**
2 teaspoons finely grated **garlic**
2 **fresh long green chillies**, halved lengthways
2 teaspoons **cumin seeds**
1 teaspoon **ground turmeric**
1 teaspoon **coriander seeds**, crushed
1 large **carrot**, coarsely grated
300 g (10 oz) **green** or **white cabbage**, finely shredded
1 tablespoon **curry powder** (see page 16)
**salt** and **pepper**

**Heat** the oil in a large nonstick wok or frying pan over a low heat. Add the shallots, ginger, garlic and chillies, and stir-fry for 2–3 minutes until the shallots have softened. Add the cumin seeds, turmeric and crushed coriander seeds, and stir-fry for 1 minute.

**Increase** the heat to high and add the carrot and cabbage, tossing well to coat in the spice mixture. Add the curry powder and season to taste. Cover the pan and cook over a medium-low heat for 10 minutes, stirring occasionally. Remove from the heat and serve immediately with steamed rice.

### For speedy coconut, carrot & cabbage curry,

heat 1 tablespoon groundnut oil in a large wok and add 2 tablespoons medium curry paste, 2 chopped garlic cloves and 1 sliced onion, and stir-fry for 3–4 minutes until softened. Chop 2 large carrots into 1 cm (½ inch) pieces and add to the onion mixture with 300 g (10 oz) roughly chopped cabbage, 300 ml (½ pint) vegetable stock and 200 ml (7 fl oz) reduced-fat coconut milk. Bring to the boil, reduce the heat to medium and cook for 12–15 minutes or until the carrot is tender. Remove from the heat and serve garnished with chopped coriander.

# lebanese tomato & courgette curry

Serves **4**

Preparation time **5 minutes**

Cooking time **40–45 minutes**

1 tablespoon **light olive oil**

1 large **onion**, finely chopped

4 **courgettes**, cut into
   1 x 3.5 cm (½ x 1½ inch)
   batons

2 x 400 g (13 oz) cans whole
   **plum tomatoes**

2 **garlic cloves**, crushed

½ teaspoon **chilli powder**

¼ teaspoon **ground turmeric**

2 teaspoons **dried mint**

**salt** and **pepper**

**mint leaves**, to garnish

**Heat** the oil in a large saucepan over a low heat. Add the onion and fry for 10–12 minutes until soft and translucent. Add the courgettes and cook for a further 5–6 minutes, stirring occasionally.

**Add** the tomatoes (including the juices) and garlic, and continue to cook over a medium heat for 20 minutes.

**Stir** in the chilli powder, turmeric and dried mint, and cook for a few more minutes to allow the flavours to mingle. Season to taste and serve with couscous or steamed white rice.

**For spicy courgette & tomato bake**, thickly slice 4 large courgettes and arrange in the base of a medium ovenproof dish. Mix a 400 g (13 oz) can chopped tomatoes with 6 tablespoons tomato purée, 100 ml (3½ fl oz) vegetable stock, 1 tablespoon hot curry powder, 2 teaspoons each of finely grated garlic and ginger, and 2 teaspoons dried mint. Season to taste and spoon over the courgettes. Cover with foil and cook in a preheated oven at 180°C (350°F), Gas Mark 4, for 25–30 minutes. Remove from the oven and serve with steamed rice.

# thai squash, tofu & pea curry

Serves **4**
Preparation time **15 minutes**
Cooking time **25 minutes**

1 tablespoon **groundnut oil**
1 tablespoon **Thai red curry paste** (see page 17)
500 g (1 lb) peeled and deseeded **butternut squash**, cubed
450 ml (¾ pint) **vegetable stock**
400 ml (14 fl oz) **reduced-fat coconut milk**
6 **kaffir lime leaves**, bruised, plus extra shredded leaves to garnish
200 g (7 oz) fresh or frozen **peas**
300 g (10 oz) **firm tofu**, diced
2 tablespoons **light soy** sauce
juice of 1 **lime**

**To garnish**
**coriander leaves**
finely chopped **fresh red chilli**

**Heat** the oil in a wok or deep frying pan, add the curry paste and stir-fry over a low heat for 1 minute. Add the squash, stir-fry briefly and then add the stock, coconut milk and lime leaves.

**Bring** to the boil, then cover, reduce the heat and simmer gently for 15 minutes until the squash is tender.

**Stir** in the peas, tofu, soy sauce and lime juice and simmer for a further 5 minutes until the peas are cooked. Spoon into serving bowls and garnish with shredded lime leaves, chopped coriander and red chilli.

**For Thai green vegetable curry**, use green curry paste (see page 19) instead of red curry paste. Replace the squash with 1 sliced carrot, 1 sliced courgette and 1 cored, deseeded and sliced red pepper and follow the recipe above.

# dry bitter melon curry

Serves **4**

Preparation time **10 minutes**, plus standing

Cooking time **25–30 minutes**

2 **bitter melons** (carilla or kerela)

1 tablespoon **ground turmeric**

1 tablespoon **groundnut oil**

1 small **onion**, halved and thinly sliced

1 tablespoon **curry powder** (see page 16)

½ teaspoon **chilli powder**

2 teaspoons **agave syrup**

3 **tomatoes**, roughly chopped

1–2 tablespoons **light soy sauce**

**sea salt**

**Scrape** the skin and blisters off the bitter melons with a vegetable peeler, just enough to remove raised parts. Cut the flesh into thin slices. Put the slices in a colander and sprinkle with sea salt. Leave to stand for 30 minutes, then rinse under cold running water to remove the bitter juices. Drain on kitchen paper and transfer to a plate. Sprinkle with the turmeric and toss to mix well.

**Heat** the oil in a large frying pan over a medium heat. Add the onion and stir-fry for 4–5 minutes. Add the curry and chilli powders, agave syrup and tomatoes, and continue to stir and cook for 8–10 minutes.

**Stir** in the bitter melon slices and cook, stirring, for 10–15 minutes. Season to taste and stir in the soy sauce. Serve immediately with rice.

**For dry okra & potato curry**, cut 500 g (1 lb) okra into 2.5 cm (1 inch) lengths. Heat 1 tablespoon groundnut oil in a large frying pan over a medium heat. Add 1 finely chopped onion and stir-fry for 4–5 minutes until soft and translucent. Add 2 tablespoons mild curry powder (see page 16), 1 teaspoon agave syrup and 3 chopped tomatoes, and continue to stir and cook for 8–10 minutes. Stir in the okra and 200 g (7 oz) boiled potato chunks. Cook over a high heat for 6–8 minutes, season and serve immediately with rice.

# spicy goan aubergine curry

Serves **4**

Preparation time **15 minutes**

Cooking time **about 25 minutes**

1 teaspoon **cumin seeds**

4 teaspoons **coriander seeds**

1 teaspoon **cayenne pepper**

2 **fresh green chillies**, deseeded and sliced

½ teaspoon **ground turmeric**

4 **garlic cloves**, crushed

1 tablespoon peeled and grated **fresh root ginger**

300 ml (½ pint) **warm water**

400 ml (14 fl oz) **reduced-fat coconut milk**

1 tablespoon **tamarind paste**

1 large **aubergine**, thinly sliced lengthways

**salt** and **pepper**

**Dry-roast** the cumin and coriander seeds in a nonstick frying pan over a low heat for 2–3 minutes until fragrant. Remove from the heat and crush them lightly. Place them in a large saucepan with the cayenne, chillies, turmeric, garlic, ginger and the measured warm water.

**Bring** to the boil, reduce the heat and simmer for 10 minutes until thickened. Season to taste. Stir in the coconut milk and tamarind paste.

**Arrange** the aubergine slices in a foil-lined grill pan and brush the tops with some of the curry sauce. Cook under a preheated hot grill, turning once, until golden and tender. Serve the aubergine slices in the curry sauce with naan bread or chapatis.

**For cashew and courgette curry**, add 200 g (7 oz) roasted cashew nuts to the finished curry sauce. To roast, soak in water for 20 minutes, chop, then heat in a dry frying pan, shaking regularly, until lightly browned. Replace the aubergine with 4 sliced courgettes and grill as above. Drizzle with walnut oil and season to taste.

# spiced potato curry

Serves **4**

Preparation time **20 minutes**

Cooking time **6−8 minutes**

1 tablespoon **groundnut oil**

1−2 teaspoons **black mustard seeds**

1 teaspoon **chilli powder** or **paprika**

4 teaspoons **cumin seeds**

8−10 **curry leaves**

2 teaspoons **ground cumin**

2 teaspoons **ground coriander**

1 teaspoon **ground turmeric**

500 g (1 lb) **potatoes**, peeled, boiled and cut into 2.5 cm (1 in) cubes

6 tablespoons chopped **coriander leaves**

4 tablespoons **lemon juice**

**salt** and **pepper**

**Heat** the oil in a large nonstick wok or frying pan over a medium-high heat. Add the mustard seeds, chilli powder, cumin seeds and curry leaves. Stir-fry for 1−2 minutes until fragrant.

**Add** the ground spices and potatoes. Season to taste and stir-fry briskly over a high heat for 4−5 minutes. Remove from the heat and stir in the coriander. Squeeze over the lemon juice just before serving.

**For quick curried spinach & potato sauté**, follow the recipe above, then after the potatoes have been stir-fried for 4−5 minutes, gently fold in 100 g (3½ oz) baby spinach. Stir-fry for 1−2 minutes, then remove from the heat, squeeze over 4 tablespoons lemon juice and serve immediately with steamed rice or bread.

# okra, pea & tomato curry

Serves **4**
Preparation time **5 minutes**
Cooking time **about
   20 minutes**

1 tablespoon **groundnut oil**
6–8 **curry leaves**
2 teaspoons **black mustard
   seeds**
1 **onion**, finely diced
2 teaspoons **ground cumin**
1 teaspoon **ground coriander**
2 teaspoons **curry powder**
1 teaspoon **ground turmeric**
3 **garlic cloves**, finely chopped
500 g (1 lb) **okra**, cut on the
   diagonal into 2.5 cm (1 inch)
   pieces
200 g (7 oz) fresh or frozen
   **peas**
2 ripe **plum tomatoes**, finely
   chopped
**salt** and **pepper**
3 tablespoons grated **fresh
   coconut**, to serve

**Heat** the oil in a large nonstick wok or frying pan over
a medium heat. Add the curry leaves, mustard seeds
and onion. Stir-fry for 3–4 minutes until fragrant and
the onion is starting to soften, then add the cumin,
coriander, curry powder and turmeric. Stir-fry for a
further 1–2 minutes until fragrant.

**Add** the garlic and okra, and increase the heat to high.
Cook, stirring, for 2–3 minutes, then add the peas
and tomatoes. Season to taste, cover and reduce the
heat to low. Cook gently for 10–12 minutes, stirring
occasionally, until the okra is just tender. Remove from
the heat and sprinkle over the grated coconut just
before serving.

**For spiced seeded pea & tomato pilaf**, place
300 g (10 oz) basmati rice in a medium saucepan with
2 teaspoons dry-roasted cumin seeds, 1 tablespoon
crushed dry-roasted coriander seeds, 2 teaspoons black
mustard seeds, 200 g (7 oz) fresh or frozen peas and
3 peeled, deseeded and finely chopped tomatoes. Add
650 ml (1 pint 2 fl oz) boiling vegetable stock, bring to
the boil and season to taste. Reduce the heat to low,
cover the pan and cook gently for 10–12 minutes or
until all the liquid has been absorbed. Remove from
the heat and allow to stand, covered and undisturbed,
for 10–15 minutes. Fluff up the grains with a fork
and serve.

# cauliflower & chickpea curry

Serves **4**
Preparation time **10 minutes**
Cooking time **about 20 minutes**

1 tablespoon **groundnut oil**
8 **spring onions,** cut into 5 cm (2 inch) lengths
2 teaspoons grated **garlic**
2 teaspoons **ground ginger**
2 tablespoons **medium curry powder** (see page 16)
300 g (10 oz) **cauliflower florets**
1 **red pepper,** cored, deseeded and diced
1 **yellow pepper,** cored, deseeded and diced
400 g (13 oz) can **chopped tomatoes**
400 g (13 oz) can **chickpeas,** rinsed and drained
**salt** and **pepper**

**Heat** the oil in a large nonstick frying pan over a medium heat. Add the spring onions and stir-fry for 2–3 minutes. Add the garlic, ginger and curry powder, and stir-fry for 20–30 seconds until fragrant. Now add the cauliflower and peppers, and stir-fry for a further 2–3 minutes.

**Stir** in the tomatoes and bring to the boil. Cover, reduce the heat to medium and simmer for 10 minutes, stirring occasionally. Add the chickpeas, season to taste and bring back to the boil. Remove from the heat and serve immediately with steamed rice and mint raita.

**For broccoli & black-eye bean curry,** follow the recipe above replacing the cauliflower with 300 g (10 oz) broccoli florets and the chickpeas with a 400 g (13 oz) can black-eye beans.

# vegetable & rice noodle laksa

Serves **4**
Preparation time **20 minutes**
Cooking time **40 minutes**

1 tablespoon **groundnut oil**
2 tablespoons finely chopped **garlic**
1 tablespoon peeled and finely chopped **fresh root ginger**
2 **fresh red chillies**, sliced
2 **onions**, finely sliced
4 tablespoons **laksa curry paste**
300 ml (10 fl oz) **vegetable stock**
250 g (8 oz) **dried rice noodles**
400 ml (14 fl oz) **reduced-fat coconut milk**
1 tablespoon **chilli bean sauce**
1 teaspoon **agave syrup**
50 g (2 oz) **bean sprouts**

**To serve**

4 **spring onions**, finely sliced
1 **fresh red chilli**, deseeded and thinly shredded
25 g (1 oz) finely chopped **coriander leaves**
3 **eggs**, hard-boiled, peeled and halved
100 g (3½ oz) roasted skinless **peanuts**, roughly chopped

**Heat** a wok or large frying pan over a high heat. Add the oil and, when it is starting to smoke, reduce the heat and add the garlic, ginger, chillies and onion. Stir-fry for 5 minutes. Add the curry paste and stock, reduce the heat to low, cover and simmer for 20 minutes.

**Meanwhile,** soak the rice noodles in a bowl of warm water for 20 minutes until tender, or according to packet instructions. Drain well.

**Add** the coconut milk to the simmering liquid in the pan. Season with the chilli bean sauce and agave syrup, and add the bean sprouts. Continue simmering for a further 15 minutes.

**Divide** the noodles between 4 warmed serving bowls and ladle the coconut broth over the top. Serve immediately with the spring onions, chilli, coriander, eggs and peanuts in individual bowls, from which diners can help themselves.

### For spicy vegetable & rice noodle stir-fry, heat
1 tablespoon groundnut oil in a large wok over a medium heat. Add 1 sliced onion, 3 thinly sliced garlic cloves, 1 teaspoon grated ginger and 2 sliced red chillies, and stir-fry for 2–3 minutes. Add a 400 g (13 oz) pack of prepared stir-fry vegetables and 300 g (10 oz) fresh rice noodles. Stir-fry for 3–4 minutes or until piping hot. Stir in 3 tablespoons light soy and 3 tablespoons sweet chilli sauce, toss to mix well and serve immediately.

# trivandrum beetroot curry

Serves **4**

Preparation time **15 minutes**

Cooking time **25–30 minutes**

1 tablespoon **groundnut oil**

1 teaspoon **black mustard seeds**

1 **onion**, chopped

2 **garlic cloves**, chopped

2 **fresh red chillies**, deseeded and finely chopped

8 **curry leaves**

1 teaspoon **ground turmeric**

1 teaspoon **cumin seeds**

1 **cinnamon stick**

400 g (13 oz) **raw beetroot**, peeled and cut into matchsticks

200 g (7 oz) canned **chopped tomatoes**

250 ml (8 fl oz) **water**

100 ml (3½ fl oz) **reduced-fat coconut milk**

juice of 1 **lime**

**salt**

chopped **coriander leaves**, to garnish

**Heat** the oil in a wok or saucepan over a medium heat. Add the mustard seeds and as soon as they begin to 'pop' (after a few seconds), add the onion, garlic and chillies. Cook for about 5 minutes until the onion is soft and translucent.

**Add** the remaining spices and the beetroot. Fry for a further 1–2 minutes, then add the tomatoes, measured water and a pinch of salt. Simmer for 15–20 minutes, stirring occasionally, until the beetroot is tender.

**Stir** in the coconut milk and simmer for a further 1–2 minutes until the sauce has thickened. Stir in the lime juice and check the seasoning. Garnish with chopped coriander and serve immediately.

**For spiced beetroot salad**, thickly slice 625 g (1¼ lb) cooked beetroot and arrange on a wide serving platter with 1 very thinly sliced red onion and a large handful of rocket leaves. Make a dressing by whisking 200 ml (7 fl oz) reduced-fat coconut milk with 1 tablespoon curry powder (see page 16) and 4 tablespoons each of very finely chopped coriander and mint. Season to taste and drizzle over the beetroot salad. Toss to mix well and serve.

# mustard, mango & yogurt curry

Serves **4**

Preparation time **20 minutes**

Cooking time **about 20 minutes**

300 g (10 oz) **fresh coconut, grated**

3–4 **fresh green chillies**, roughly chopped

1 tablespoon **cumin seeds**

500 ml (17 fl oz) **water**

3 firm, ripe **mangoes**, peeled, stoned and cubed

1 teaspoon **ground turmeric**

1 teaspoon **chilli powder**

300 ml (½ pint) **fat-free natural yogurt,** lightly whisked

1 tablespoon **groundnut oil**

2 teaspoons **black mustard seeds**

3–4 hot **dried red chillies**

10–12 **curry leaves**

**Place** the coconut, green chillies and cumin seeds in a food processor with half the measured water and blend to a fine paste.

**Place** the mangoes in a heavy saucepan with the turmeric, chilli powder and the remaining measured water. Bring to the boil, add the coconut paste and stir to mix well. Cover and simmer over a medium heat for 10–12 minutes, stirring occasionally, until the mixture becomes fairly thick.

**Add** the yogurt and heat gently, stirring, until just warmed through. Do not let the mixture come to the boil or it will curdle. Remove from the heat and keep warm.

**Heat** the oil in a small pan over a medium-high heat. Add the mustard seeds and as soon as they begin to 'pop' (after a few seconds), add the dried chillies and curry leaves. Stir-fry for a few seconds until the chillies darken. Stir the spice mixture into the mango curry and serve immediately.

**For spicy mango & mint salad**, peel, stone and cube 4 ripe mangoes. Place in a serving dish with ½ thinly sliced red onion, 12 halved cherry tomatoes and a large handful of mint leaves. Make a dressing by whisking 200 ml (7 fl oz) fat-free natural yogurt with the juice of 1 lime, 1 teaspoon agave syrup and 1 finely diced red chilli. Season, drizzle over the salad, toss to mix well and serve.

# lime leaf & cashew nut curry

Serves **4**
Preparation time **10 minutes**
Cooking time **50 minutes**

600 ml (1 pint) **reduced-fat coconut milk**
1 **onion,** chopped
1 teaspoon peeled and finely grated **fresh root ginger**
1 teaspoon peeled and finely grated **galangal**
2 fresh **green chillies,** deseeded and finely chopped
10 **kaffir lime leaves**
1 **cinnamon stick**
1 teaspoon **ground turmeric**
250 g (8 oz) raw **cashew nuts**
200 g (7 oz) fresh or frozen **peas**
2 tablespoons chopped **coriander leaves**, to garnish

**Place** the coconut milk, onion, ginger, galangal, chilli, lime leaves, cinnamon stick and turmeric in a medium saucepan and bring to the boil. Reduce the heat and simmer for 20 minutes.

**Add** the cashew nuts and cook for a further 20 minutes or until the nuts are tender. Add the peas and cook for 3–4 minutes. Remove the curry from the heat and discard the cinnamon stick and lime leaves. Scatter the coriander over the curry and serve hot with jasmine rice and pickles.

**For toasted spicy cashew nuts**, place 500 g (1 lb) whole roasted cashew nuts on an ungreased baking sheet and cook in a preheated oven at 180°C (350°F), Gas Mark 4, for about 10 minutes or until they are warmed through. Meanwhile, mix together 1 tablespoon medium curry powder (see page 16), 1 tablespoon sweet smoked paprika and 2 teaspoons crushed dried curry leaves and season with sea salt. Toss the warm nuts with the spice mixture until completely coated. Serve warm as a snack or cocktail accompaniment.

# laotian mushroom & tofu curry

Serves **4**
Preparation time **15 minutes**
Cooking time **about 1 hour**

1 tablespoon **groundnut oil**
6 **shallots**, roughly chopped
1 **garlic clove**, chopped
4 cm (1½ inch) piece of **fresh
    root ginger**, peeled and
    thinly sliced
2 **lemon grass stalks**, cut into
    5 cm (2 inch) pieces (tough
    outer leaves removed)
1 tablespoon **mild curry
    powder** (see page 16)
1 **red pepper**, cored,
    deseeded and roughly
    chopped
2 large **carrots**, sliced on the
    diagonal
400 g (13 oz) large **button
    mushrooms**, thickly sliced
250 g (8 oz) **firm tofu**, cubed
900 ml (1½ pints) **vegetable
    stock**
400 ml (14 fl oz) **reduced-fat
    coconut milk**
**salt** and **pepper**
50 g (2 oz) **bean sprouts**, to
    garnish

**Heat** the oil in a large saucepan over a medium heat.
Add the shallots and cook for 5 minutes until soft and
translucent. Stir in the garlic, ginger, lemon grass and
curry powder. Gently fry for a further 5 minutes until
fragrant.

**Add** the red pepper, carrots, mushrooms and tofu, and
stir well. Pour in the stock and season to taste. Bring to
the boil, then stir in the coconut milk. Bring to the boil
again, reduce the heat and simmer for 45–50 minutes
until the vegetables are tender.

**Ladle** the curry into warmed serving bowls, garnish
each bowl with a pile of bean sprouts and serve with
steamed rice or bread.

**For mushroom & tofu stir-fry**, mix 2 tablespoons
dark soy sauce with 2 tablespoons oyster sauce,
1 tablespoon lemon grass paste, 1 teaspoon honey
and 2 tablespoons Chinese rice wine or dry sherry and
set aside. Heat 1 tablespoon groundnut oil in a large
nonstick wok. Add 200 g (7 oz) canned bamboo shoots,
drained, and 400 g (13 oz) sliced shiitake mushrooms.
Stir-fry for 6–7 minutes or until the mushrooms are
softened and lightly browned. Add 250 g (8 oz) diced
firm tofu and the soy sauce mixture. Stir-fry until piping
hot and serve immediately.

# paneer curry

Serves **4**
Preparation time **20 minutes**
Cooking time **about 30 minutes**

1 tablespoon **groundnut oil**
8 **shallots**, finely chopped
2 tablespoons **curry powder** (see page 16)
4 ripe **plum tomatoes**, roughly chopped
2 teaspoons finely grated **garlic**
2 **fresh red chillies**, deseeded and finely sliced
2 tablespoons **tomato purée**
1 teaspoon **palm sugar** or **brown sugar**
150 ml (¼ pint) **water**
200 ml (7 fl oz) **tomato passata**
500 g (1 lb) **paneer** (Indian cottage cheese), cubed
200 g (7 oz) fresh or frozen **peas**
**salt** and **pepper**
6 tablespoons finely chopped **coriander leaves**

**Heat** the oil in a large nonstick wok over a medium-high heat. Add the shallots and stir-fry for 2–3 minutes. Sprinkle over the curry powder and stir-fry for a further 1 minute until fragrant.

**Add** the tomatoes, garlic, chillies, tomato purée, sugar and measured water, and bring to the boil. Reduce the heat to low and simmer, uncovered, for 15–20 minutes.

**Stir** in the passata, paneer and peas, and simmer gently for 5 minutes or until the paneer is heated through and the peas are cooked. Season to taste, remove from the heat and stir in the chopped coriander just before serving.

**For spicy paneer bruschetta**, finely grate 300 g (10 oz) paneer into a bowl and add 4 finely diced shallots, ½ peeled, deseeded and finely diced cucumber, 1 finely chopped green chilli, a small handful of finely chopped coriander leaves, 2 tablespoons light olive oil and the juice of 2 limes. Season to taste and toss to mix. Lightly toast 12 thick slices of ciabatta bread and place on a serving plate. Spoon the paneer mixture on to the toast and serve immediately.

# south indian vegetable stew

Serves **4**

Preparation time **15 minutes**

Cooking time **20–25 minutes**

1 tablespoon **groundnut oil**

6 **shallots**, halved and thinly sliced

2 teaspoons **black mustard seeds**

8–10 **curry leaves**

1 **fresh green chilli**, thinly sliced

2 teaspoons peeled and finely grated **fresh root ginger**

1 teaspoon **ground turmeric**

2 teaspoons **ground cumin**

6 **black peppercorns**

2 **carrots**, cut into thick batons

1 **courgette**, cut into thick batons

200 g (7 oz) **French beans**, trimmed

1 **potato**, peeled and cut into thin batons

400 ml (14 fl oz) **reduced-fat coconut milk**

400 ml (14 fl oz) **vegetable stock**

2 tablespoons **lemon juice**

**salt** and **pepper**

**Heat** the oil in a large frying pan over a medium heat. Add the shallots and stir-fry for 4–5 minutes. Add the mustard seeds, curry leaves, chilli, ginger, turmeric, cumin and peppercorns, and stir-fry for a further 1–2 minutes until fragrant.

**Add** the carrots, courgette, beans and potato to the pan. Pour in the coconut milk and stock and bring to the boil. Reduce the heat to low, cover and simmer gently for 12–15 minutes until the vegetables are tender. Season to taste, remove from the heat and squeeze over the lemon juice just before serving.

**For spicy tomato, vegetable & coconut curry**, follow the recipe above, replacing the turmeric, cumin and black peppercorns with 2 tablespoons hot curry powder (see page 16), and the vegetable stock with 400 ml (14 fl oz) tomato passata. Serve with steamed white rice.

# tindori & lentil curry

Serves **4**
Preparation time **15 minutes**
Cooking time **35 minutes**

125 g (4 oz) **green lentils**,
  rinsed
1 tablespoon **groundnut oil**
1 teaspoon **ground turmeric**
2 teaspoons **garam masala**
1 teaspoon **cumin seeds**
1 teaspoon **nigella seeds**
1 **fresh red chilli**, finely
  chopped
1 **fresh green chilli**, finely
  chopped
3 large **tomatoes**, chopped
250 g (8 oz) **tindori**, rinsed
  and trimmed
2 tablespoons **palm sugar** or
  **brown sugar**
1 tablespoon **tamarind paste**
150 ml (¼ pint) **boiling water**
**salt** and **pepper**

**Cook** the lentils in a saucepan of boiling water for
20 minutes until soft. Drain well.

**Meanwhile,** heat the oil in a large saucepan and fry the
turmeric, garam masala, cumin seeds and nigella seeds
for 1–2 minutes or until the spices are sizzling. Add the
chopped chillies, tomatoes, lentils and tindori and bring
to the boil. Cover the pan, reduce the heat and simmer
gently for 10 minutes, stirring occasionally.

**Mix** the sugar and tamarind paste with the boiling water
and add to the pan. Stir well and simmer for a further
5 minutes. Season to taste and serve with chapatis.

**For green mango & red onion salad**, to serve as an
accompaniment, peel and stone 1 small green mango
and finely shred the flesh. Mix with 1 small finely
chopped red onion and a handful of coriander leaves.
Cover and chill until required.

# watermelon & pumpkin seed curry

Serves **4**
Preparation time **15 minutes**
Cooking time **6–7 minutes**

2 tablespoons **groundnut oil**
2 large **garlic cloves**, crushed
2 teaspoons **fennel seeds**
1 teaspoon **nigella seeds**
1 teaspoon **paprika**
1 teaspoon **ground turmeric**
1 small **watermelon**, peeled,
  deseeded and cut into 2 cm
  (¾ inch) cubes
juice of 1 **lime**
8 tablespoons **pumpkin
  seeds**, toasted
**salt**
small handful of roughly
  chopped **mint leaves**,
  to garnish

**Heat** the oil in a large saucepan over a medium heat. Add the garlic, fennel and nigella seeds, paprika and turmeric, and stir-fry for 1 minute until fragrant.

**Add** the watermelon and stir-fry for 4–5 minutes. Remove from the heat, season to taste and add the lime juice and pumpkin seeds. Toss to mix well and serve immediately with the mint scattered over the top.

**For minted watermelon, lime & ginger cooler**, place the deseeded flesh of 1 small watermelon in a food processor with 1 teaspoon grated ginger, the finely grated rind and juice of 2 limes, 4 tablespoons agave syrup and a small handful of finely chopped mint leaves. Blend until smooth and divide between 4 tall glasses filled with crushed ice.

# rice, pulses & grains

# prawn & coriander pilaf

Serves **4**
Preparation time **10 minutes**
Cooking time **20–30 minutes**

1 tablespoon **groundnut oil**
1 large **onion**, finely chopped
1 fresh **red chilli**, deseeded
  and finely diced
2 **garlic cloves**, finely chopped
2 tablespoons fresh **curry
  paste** (see below)
250 g (8 oz) **basmati rice**
600 ml (1 pint) **fish stock**
finely grated rind and juice of
  1 large **lime**
20 g (¾ oz) **coriander leaves**,
  finely chopped
300 g (10 oz) cooked peeled
  **prawns**
**salt** and **pepper**

**Heat** the oil in a large saucepan over a medium heat. Add the onion and gently fry for 4–5 minutes. Add the chilli, garlic and curry paste, and stir-fry for 1–2 minutes until fragrant, then add the rice and mix well.

**Pour** in the stock and add the lime rind. Season to taste, cover the pan and simmer gently for 15–20 minutes until the stock has been absorbed and the rice is cooked.

**Stir** in the lime juice, coriander and prawns. Allow the prawns to warm through, then serve immediately.

**For homemade fresh curry paste**, place 2 sliced green chillies in a mini blender with 6 chopped garlic cloves, 1 teaspoon ground cardamom, 2 teaspoons grated ginger, 2 tablespoons grated fresh coconut, 1 teaspoon ground turmeric, 2 cloves, 2 teaspoons cumin seeds, a large handful of finely chopped coriander leaves, 2 tablespoons malt or white wine vinegar, the juice of 1 lime and 100 ml (3½ fl oz) water. Blend to a smooth paste, adding more water if necessary. Store any leftover paste in an airtight jar in the refrigerator for up to 1 week, or freeze in small portions for later use.

# chickpea & red pepper curry

Serves **4**

Preparation time **10 minutes**

Cooking time **40–45 minutes**

1 tablespoon **groundnut oil**

4 **garlic cloves**, crushed

2 teaspoons peeled and finely grated **fresh root ginger**

1 large **onion**, coarsely grated

1–2 **fresh green chillies**, finely sliced

1 teaspoon **hot chilli powder**

1 tablespoon **ground cumin**

1 tablespoon **ground coriander**

3 tablespoons **fat-free natural yogurt**, plus extra to drizzle

4 tablespoons **tomato purée**

2 teaspoons **garam masala**

500 ml (17 fl oz) **water**

2 teaspoons **tamarind paste**

2 teaspoons **medium curry powder** (see page 16)

1 **red pepper**, cored, deseeded and cubed

2 x 400 g (13 oz) cans **chickpeas**, rinsed and drained

**salt**

chopped **coriander leaves**, to garnish

**lemon wedges**, to serve

**Heat** the oil in a large frying pan over a medium heat. Add the garlic, ginger, onion and chillies and stir-fry for 6–8 minutes until the onion is lightly golden. Add the chilli powder, cumin, ground coriander, yogurt, tomato purée and garam masala. Stir-fry for a further 1–2 minutes.

**Add** the measured water and bring to the boil. Add the tamarind paste, curry powder, red pepper and chickpeas, and bring back to the boil. Season to taste, reduce the heat to low and simmer gently for 25–30 minutes until the sauce is thick and rich.

**Divide** between 4 small serving bowls, drizzle with extra yogurt and garnish with chopped coriander. Serve with lemon wedges on the side.

**For chickpea & red pepper pilau**, heat 1 tablespoon groundnut oil in a large saucepan over a medium heat. Add 1 finely chopped onion and fry for 5 minutes until soft. Add 1 finely diced red pepper and 1 chopped garlic clove, and continue frying for 2 minutes. Stir in 300 g (10 oz) basmati rice, 400 g (13 oz) can chickpeas, rinsed and drained, and 1 tablespoon medium curry powder, and stir-fry for 1 minute. Add 650 ml (1 pint 2 fl oz) boiling water, season to taste and bring to the boil. Reduce the heat to low, cover the pan and cook gently for 10–12 minutes or until all the liquid has been absorbed. Remove from the heat and allow to stand, covered and undisturbed, for 10–15 minutes. Fluff up the grains with a fork and serve.

# spinach & mung bean dhal

Serves **4**

Preparation time **10 minutes**, plus soaking

Cooking time **about 40 minutes**

200 g (7 oz) **dried split yellow mung beans** (moong dhal), rinsed

1.5 litres (2½ pints) **water**

1 teaspoon **asafoetida**

1 teaspoon **ground turmeric**

175 g (6 oz) **baby spinach**, roughly chopped

12–15 **cherry tomatoes**

small handful of finely chopped **coriander leaves**

1 tablespoon **groundnut oil**

2 teaspoons **cumin seeds**

2 teaspoons **black mustard seeds**

2 **fresh green chillies**, deseeded and finely sliced

1 tablespoon **ground coriander**

1 tablespoon **ground cumin**

2 tablespoons finely chopped **garlic**

2 tablespoons peeled and finely chopped **fresh root ginger**

**salt**

**Place** the mung beans in a bowl and cover with cold water. Leave to soak for 5–6 hours or overnight. Transfer to a colander and rinse under cold running water. Drain and place in a medium saucepan with the measured water. Add the asafoetida and turmeric, and bring to the boil. Boil rapidly for 10 minutes, then reduce the heat to low. Simmer gently for 10–15 minutes, skimming off any scum that rises to the surface and stirring often.

**Use** a balloon whisk to whisk the mixture until fairly smooth. Add the spinach and stir to mix well. Stir in the tomatoes and cook over a medium heat for 10–12 minutes, stirring often. Remove from the heat and stir in the chopped coriander.

**Heat** the oil in a small frying pan over a high heat. When hot, add the cumin seeds, mustard seeds, chilli, ground coriander, ground cumin, garlic and ginger. Stir-fry for 30–40 seconds, then tip the contents of the pan into the dhal. Stir to mix well and season to taste. Serve hot.

**For spiced gram flour flatbreads**, to serve as an accompaniment, sift 115 g (3 ¾ oz) each of wholemeal flour and gram flour with 1 teaspoon salt into a bowl. Add 2 teaspoons cumin seeds, 1 teaspoon ground turmeric, 3 tablespoons groundnut oil and 2 tablespoons chopped coriander leaves. Mix well and gradually add about 200 ml (7 fl oz) water to form a soft dough. Knead on a lightly floured surface for 1–2 minutes, then allow to rest for 10 minutes. Divide the mixture into 8 and roll out each piece to a 15 cm (6 inch) round. Brush the tops with a little oil. Heat a nonstick frying pan over a high heat. When hot, cook the breads, one at a time, for 35–40 seconds on each side, pressing down with a spatula for even cooking.

# cauliflower & turkey biryani

Serves **4**
Preparation time **25 minutes**
Cooking time **40 minutes**

300 g (10 oz) **turkey breast**,
  cubed
4 tablespoons **groundnut oil**
2 **onions**, thinly sliced
1 small **cauliflower**, cut into
  small florets
2 **bay leaves**
300 g (10 oz) **basmati rice**
750 ml (1 ¼ pints) **chicken
  stock**
1 tablespoon **nigella seeds**
**salt** and **pepper**
2 tablespoons **flaked
  almonds**, toasted, to garnish

**Marinade**
1 **onion**, roughly chopped
2 **garlic cloves**, chopped
25 g (1 oz) **fresh root ginger**,
  peeled and roughly chopped
2 teaspoons **ground turmeric**
¼ teaspoon **ground cloves**
½ teaspoon **dried chilli flakes**
¼ teaspoon **ground cinnamon**
2 teaspoons **medium curry
  paste**
1 tablespoon **lemon juice**
2 teaspoons **sugar**

**Place** all the marinade ingredients in a food processor, blend to a thick paste and turn into a large bowl. Add the turkey, season to taste, mix well and set aside.

**Heat** 3 tablespoons of the oil in a large frying pan and fry half the sliced onion until deep golden and crisp. Remove with a slotted spoon and drain on kitchen paper.

**Add** the cauliflower to the frying pan and fry gently for 5 minutes. Add the remaining onion and cook, stirring, for about 5 minutes until the cauliflower is softened and golden. Drain on kitchen paper.

**Heat** the remaining oil in the pan. Add the turkey and marinade and fry gently for 5 minutes, stirring. Add the bay leaves, rice and stock and bring to the boil. Reduce the heat and simmer very gently, stirring occasionally, for 10–12 minutes until the rice is tender and the stock has been absorbed, adding a little water if the mixture is dry before the rice is cooked. Stir in the nigella seeds and cauliflower and heat through. Garnish with the crisp onion and toasted almonds and serve immediately.

**For cucumber & mint raita**, to serve as an accompaniment, place 175 ml (6 fl oz) fat-free natural yogurt in a bowl with 75 g (3 oz) deseeded and grated cucumber, 2 tablespoons chopped mint, a pinch of ground cumin, and lemon juice and salt to taste. Stand for 30 minutes before serving.

# lamb & red rice pilaf

Serves **3–4**
Preparation time **20 minutes**
Cooking time **1¼ hours**

10 **cardamom pods**
2 teaspoons **cumin seeds**
2 teaspoons **coriander seeds**
2 tablespoons **light olive oil**
500 g (1 lb) **lean shoulder of lamb**, trimmed and diced
2 **red onions**, sliced
25 g (1 oz) **fresh root ginger**, peeled and grated
2 **garlic cloves**, crushed
½ teaspoon **ground turmeric**
200 g (7 oz) **red rice**
600 ml (1 pint) **lamb stock** (see below)
40 g (1½ oz) **pine nuts**
75 g (3 oz) **soft dried apricots**, thinly sliced
50 g (2 oz) **rocket**
**salt** and **pepper**

**Preheat** the oven to 180°C (350°F), Gas Mark 4. Crush the cardamom pods to release the seeds, then roughly grind the seeds in a pestle and mortar with the cumin and coriander. Discard the pods.

**Heat** the oil in a small, sturdy roasting tin and fry the spices for 30 seconds. Add the lamb and onions and toss with the spices. Cook in the preheated oven for 40 minutes until the lamb and onions are browned.

**Return** to the hob and stir in the ginger, garlic, turmeric and rice. Add the stock and bring to the boil. Cover with a lid or foil and cook over the lowest setting for about 30 minutes until the rice is tender and the stock has been absorbed.

**Stir** in the pine nuts and apricots and season to taste. Scatter with the rocket and fold in very lightly. Pile on to serving plates and serve immediately.

**For homemade lamb stock**, place 750 g (1½lb) roasted lamb bones and meat scraps in a large saucepan with 1 large onion, roughly chopped, 2 large carrots and 2 celery sticks, both roughly sliced, 1 teaspoon black peppercorns and several bay leaves and thyme sprigs. Just cover with cold water and bring slowly to the boil. Reduce the heat and simmer for 3 hours, skimming the surface if necessary. Strain through a sieve and leave to cool. Store for up to 1 week in the refrigerator, or freeze for later use.

# black lentil curry

Serves **4**

Preparation time **20 minutes**, plus soaking

Cooking time **about 1 hour**

125 g (4 oz) **dried whole black lentils**, rinsed and drained

1 litre (1¾ pints) **water**

1 tablespoon **groundnut oil**

1 **onion**, finely chopped

3 **garlic cloves**, crushed

2 teaspoons peeled and finely grated **fresh root ginger**

1 **fresh green chilli**, halved lengthways

2 teaspoons **cumin seeds**

1 teaspoon **ground coriander**

1 teaspoon **ground turmeric**

1 teaspoon **paprika**, plus extra for sprinkling

200 g (7 oz) canned **red kidney beans**, rinsed and drained

large handful of chopped **coriander leaves**

**salt**

200 ml (7 fl oz) **fat-free natural yogurt**, whisked, to serve

**Place** the lentils in a deep bowl and cover with cold water. Leave to soak for 10–12 hours. Transfer to a colander and rinse under cold running water. Drain and place in a saucepan with half the measured water. Bring to the boil, reduce the heat to low and simmer for 35–40 minutes until tender. Drain and set aside.

**Heat** the oil in a large saucepan over a medium heat. Add the onion, garlic, ginger, chilli, cumin seeds and ground coriander, and stir-fry for 5–6 minutes until the onion is soft and translucent. Add the turmeric, paprika, kidney beans and lentils, and stir thoroughly.

**Add** the remaining measured water and bring back to the boil. Reduce the heat to low and simmer gently for 10–15 minutes, stirring often. Remove from the heat and season to taste. Stir in the coriander and sprinkle over a little extra paprika. Serve immediately with the yogurt.

**For wholemeal parathas**, to serve as an accompaniment, sift 225 g (7½ oz) wholemeal flour and 100 g (3½ oz) plain flour into a large bowl, and add 1 teaspoon ground cardamom and 1 teaspoon salt. Make a well in the centre and pour in 250 ml (8 fl oz) warmed buttermilk and 2 tablespoons groundnut oil. Work together to make a soft dough. Knead on a lightly floured surface for 10 minutes and form into a ball. Place in a bowl, cover with a damp cloth and leave to rest for 20 minutes. Divide the dough into 12 balls, and roll each one out to a 15 cm (6 inch) round. Heat a nonstick frying pan over a medium heat. Brush each paratha with a little oil, fold in half, then brush again. Fold in half once more to form a triangle, dust with a little flour and flatten with a rolling pin to a 15 cm (6 inch) triangle. Cook in the hot pan for 1 minute on each side.

# chicken & pickled walnut pilaf

Serves **4**
Preparation time **20 minutes**
Cooking time **35 minutes**

400 g (13 oz) skinless,
   boneless **chicken thighs**,
   chopped
2 teaspoons **Moroccan spice
   mix** (see below)
2 tablespoons **light olive oil**
25 g (1 oz) **pine nuts**
1 large **onion**, chopped
3 **garlic cloves**, sliced
½ teaspoon **ground turmeric**
250 g (8 oz) **mixed long-
   grain and wild rice**
300 ml (½ pint) **chicken stock**
3 pieces of **stem ginger**, finely
   chopped
3 tablespoons chopped
   **parsley**
2 tablespoons chopped **mint
   leaves**
50 g (2 oz) **pickled walnuts**,
   sliced
**salt** and **pepper**

**Toss** the chicken with the spice mix and a little salt to coat. Heat the oil in a large frying pan and cook the pine nuts until they begin to colour. Drain with a slotted spoon. Add the chicken to the pan and fry gently for 6–8 minutes, stirring until lightly browned.

**Add** the onion and fry gently for 5 minutes. Add the garlic and turmeric and fry for a further 1 minute. Add the rice and stock and bring to the boil. Reduce the heat to low and simmer very gently for about 15 minutes until the rice is tender and the stock absorbed. Add a little water if the liquid has been absorbed before the rice is cooked.

**Stir** in the ginger, parsley, mint, walnuts and pine nuts. Season to taste and heat through gently for 2 minutes before serving.

**For homemade Moroccan spice mix**, combine ½ teaspoon each of crushed fennel seeds, cumin seeds, coriander seeds and mustard seeds with ¼ teaspoon each of ground cloves and cinnamon.

# tamarind & red lentil curry

Serves **4**

Preparation time **10 minutes**

Cooking time **about 50 minutes**

250 g (8 oz) **dried red lentils** (masoor dhal), rinsed

1 teaspoon **ground turmeric**

1 litre (1¾ pints) **boiling water**

1 tablespoon **groundnut oil**

1 teaspoon **black mustard seeds**

1 tablespoon **medium curry powder** (see page 16)

4 **hot dried red chillies**

1 **bay leaf**

150 ml (5 fl oz) **water**

2 teaspoons **tamarind paste**

1 teaspoon **agave syrup**

small handful of chopped **coriander leaves**

**salt**

**Place** lentils and turmeric in a medium saucepan with the measured boiling water and bring to the boil. Reduce the heat to low and simmer gently for 40 minutes, skimming off any scum that rises to the surface and stirring often. Use a balloon whisk to whisk the mixture until fairly smooth.

**Heat** the oil in a wok or frying pan over a medium heat. Add the mustard seeds and as soon as they begin to 'pop' (after a few seconds), add the curry powder, chillies and bay leaf. Stir-fry for 5–6 seconds until the chillies darken in colour.

**Add** the cooked lentils and measured water, and season to taste. Stir to mix through. Add the tamarind paste and agave syrup, and bring to the boil. Reduce the heat to low and simmer gently for 8–10 minutes. Stir in the coriander and serve immediately.

**For tomato rice**, to serve as an accompaniment, heat 1 tablespoon groundnut oil in a large saucepan over a medium heat, and fry 2 sliced shallots, 2 sliced garlic cloves and 2 teaspoons cumin seeds for 4–5 minutes until soft and fragrant. Add 4 peeled, deseeded and finely diced tomatoes and 300 g (10 oz) basmati rice, and stir-fry for 2–3 minutes. Season to taste and add 650 ml (1 pint 2 fl oz) boiling water. Bring to the boil, reduce the heat to low, cover the pan and cook gently for 10–12 minutes or until all the liquid has been absorbed. Remove from the heat and allow to stand, covered and undisturbed, for 10–15 minutes. Fluff up the grains with a fork and serve.

# punjabi kidney bean curry

Serves **4**

Preparation time **10 minutes**, plus soaking

Cooking time **about 1 hour**

200 g (7 oz) **dried red kidney beans**

1 tablespoon **groundnut oil**

1 **onion**, finely chopped

5 cm (2 inch) **cinnamon stick**

2 **dried bay leaves**

4 **garlic cloves**, crushed

2 teaspoons peeled and finely grated **fresh root ginger**

1 teaspoon **ground coriander**

2 teaspoons **ground cumin**

2 tablespoons **medium curry powder** (see page 16)

400 g (13 oz) can **chopped tomatoes**

250 ml (8 fl oz) **boiling water**

**salt** and **pepper**

**To serve**

200 ml (7 fl oz) **fat-free natural yogurt**, whisked

small handful of chopped **coriander leaves**

**Place** the beans in a deep bowl and cover with cold water. Leave to soak overnight. Place in a large saucepan with double the volume of water and bring to the boil. Boil rapidly for 10 minutes, then reduce the heat to low. Simmer gently for about 40 minutes until the beans are tender.

**Meanwhile,** heat the oil in a large saucepan over a medium heat. Add the onion, cinnamon, bay leaf, garlic and ginger, and stir-fry for 4–5 minutes. Add the ground coriander, cumin and curry powder, and stir to mix well.

**Drain** the beans and add to the saucepan with the tomatoes and measured boiling water. Bring to the boil, reduce the heat and simmer for 10 minutes, stirring often. Remove from the heat and season to taste. Swirl in the whisked yogurt and coriander just before serving.

**For homemade naan breads**, to serve as an accompaniment, sift 450 g (14½ oz) self-raising wholemeal flour, 2 teaspoons sugar, 1 teaspoon salt and 1 teaspoon baking powder into a large bowl. Add 3 tablespoons groundnut oil and rub into the flour. Gradually add 250 ml (8 fl oz) warm skimmed milk, and mix to a soft dough. Knead on a lightly floured work surface for 6–8 minutes until smooth. Put back in the bowl, cover and rest for 20–25 minutes. Divide the mixture into 8 balls and roll each one out into a thick cake. Cover and set aside for 10–15 minutes. Preheat the grill to medium-high. Roll each piece into a 23 cm (9 inch) disc, brush the tops with oil and sprinkle with nigella seeds. Cooking in batches, place the breads on a lightly oiled grill rack and cook under the grill for 1–2 minutes on each side until puffed and browned in spots.

# spiced rice with lentils

Serves **4**

Preparation time **20 minutes**, plus standing

Cooking time **20–25 minutes**

125 g (4 oz) **red split lentils**

225 g (7 1/2 oz) **basmati rice**

3 tablespoons **sunflower oil**

1 **onion**, finely chopped

1 teaspoon **ground turmeric**

1 tablespoon **cumin seeds**

1 **dried red chilli**

1 **cinnamon stick**

3 **cloves**

3 **cardamom pods**, lightly bruised

500 ml (17 fl oz) **vegetable stock**

8 **cherry tomatoes**, halved

6 tablespoons finely chopped **coriander leaves**

**salt** and **pepper**

**crispy fried onions**, to garnish

**Wash** the lentils and rice several times in cold water. Drain thoroughly.

**Heat** the oil in a heavy-based saucepan and add the onion. Stir-fry for 6—8 minutes over a medium heat and then add the spices.

**Continue** to stir-fry for 2—3 minutes, then add the rice and lentils. Stir-fry for another 2—3 minutes, then add the stock, tomatoes and fresh coriander. Season well and bring to the boil. Reduce the heat, cover tightly and simmer for 10 minutes.

**Remove** the pan from the heat and allow to stand undisturbed for another 10 minutes. Transfer to a serving dish and garnish with crispy fried onions. Serve immediately with pickles and natural yogurt, if liked.

**For spiced rice with yellow split peas**, use the same quantity of yellow split peas instead of red lentils – they can be treated in exactly the same way. Proceed as above.

# balinese vegetable fried rice

Serves **4**
Preparation time **15 minutes**
Cooking time **10–15 minutes**

1 **courgette**, cut into thick
batons
1 **carrot**, cut into matchsticks
200 g (7 oz) **French beans**,
halved
1 tablespoon **groundnut oil**,
plus extra for greasing
6 **spring onions**, thinly sliced
on the diagonal
3 **garlic cloves**, thinly sliced
1 teaspoon **ground coriander**
1 teaspoon **medium curry
powder** (see page 16)
½ **red pepper**, cored,
deseeded and sliced
½ **yellow pepper**, cored,
deseeded and sliced
400 g (13 oz) cold cooked
**long-grain rice**
2 tablespoons **light soy sauce**
2 large **eggs**
1 tablespoon finely chopped
**coriander leaves**, plus extra
to garnish
1 tablespoon **water**
**salt** and **pepper**
**mint leaves**, to garnish

**Blanch** the courgette, carrot and beans in a large
saucepan of lightly salted boiling water for 2 minutes.
Drain and set aside.

**Heat** the oil in a large wok or frying pan with a lid over a
medium heat and add the spring onions, garlic, ground
coriander and curry powder. Stir-fry for 2–3 minutes, then
add the peppers and stir-fry for another minute. Add the
rice and vegetables and stir-fry for 3–4 minutes, then stir
in the soy sauce. Toss to mix well, and season to taste.
Remove from the heat, cover and keep warm.

**Grease** a medium nonstick frying pan with oil and place
over a low heat. Whisk the eggs with the coriander
leaves and measured water. Pour the egg mixture into
the pan and swirl around. Cook gently for 1–2 minutes
until the bottom is set, then carefully turn over and cook
for another minute. Turn out on to a board and cut into
thin strips.

**Divide** the rice between 4 warmed plates and top with
the omelette strips. Serve immediately, garnished with
extra coriander and mint leaves.

**For quick vegetable curry fried rice**, blanch a 400 g
(13 oz) bag of frozen, diced mixed vegetables in a
saucepan of lightly salted boiling water for 2 minutes,
then drain well. Heat 1 tablespoon groundnut oil in a
large, nonstick wok and add 2 tablespoons Thai green
curry paste (see page 17). Stir-fry for 30 seconds,
then add 500 g (1 lb) cooked basmati rice and the
vegetables. Stir-fry over a high heat for 4–5 minutes,
add 50 ml (2 fl oz) reduced-fat coconut milk and heat
until piping hot. Season and serve.

# dhal makhani with kidney beans

Serves **4**

Preparation time **20 minutes,**
  plus soaking

Cooking time **about 50
  minutes**

125 g (4 oz) **dried split black
  lentils**, rinsed and drained

500 ml (17 fl oz) **boiling water**

1 tablespoon **groundnut oil**

1 **onion**, finely chopped

3 **garlic cloves**, crushed

2 teaspoons finely grated
  **fresh root ginger**

2 **fresh green chillies**, halved
  lengthways

1 teaspoon **ground turmeric**

1 teaspoon **paprika**, plus extra
  for sprinkling

1 tablespoon **ground cumin**

1 tablespoon **ground
  coriander**

200 g (7 oz) canned **red
  kidney beans**

500 ml (17 fl oz) **water**

200 g (7 oz) **baby spinach**

large handful of chopped
  **coriander leaves**

**salt**

200 ml (7 fl oz) **fat-free
  natural yogurt**, whisked,
  to serve

**Place** the lentils in a deep bowl and cover with cold water. Leave to soak for 10–12 hours. Transfer to a colander and rinse under cold running water. Drain and place in a medium saucepan with the measured boiling water. Bring to the boil, then reduce the heat to low. Simmer gently for 35–40 minutes, skimming off any scum that rises to the surface and stirring often.

**Meanwhile,** heat the oil in a large saucepan and add the onion, garlic, ginger and chillies. Stir-fry for 5–6 minutes and then add the turmeric, paprika, cumin, ground coriander, kidney beans and lentils.

**Add** the measured water and bring to the boil. Reduce the heat and stir in the spinach. Cook gently for 10–15 minutes, stirring often. Remove from the heat and season to taste. Stir in the chopped coriander and drizzle over the yogurt. Sprinkle with a little paprika and serve immediately with parathas.

**For dhal makhani with black beans**, follow the recipe above but replace the kidney beans with a 425 g (14 oz) can black beans, rinsed and drained. Replace the baby spinach with 150 g (5 oz) white cabbage, finely shredded, for a more substantial texture.

# tamarind rice

Serves **4**
Preparation time **10 minutes**
Cooking time **about 20 minutes**

1 tablespoon **sunflower oil**
1 large **red onion**, thinly sliced
2 **aubergines**, cut into cubes
1 **fresh red chilli**, deseeded
  and thinly sliced
2 tablespoons **tamarind paste**
1 tablespoon **dark muscovado sugar**
500 g (1 lb) cooked **basmati rice**
8 tablespoons **fresh mint leaves**, roughly chopped
200 g (7 oz) **baby spinach leaves**
**salt** and **pepper**

**Warm** the oil in a large frying pan over a medium heat. Add the sliced onion and cook for 10 minutes or until lightly browned.

**Increase** the heat to high. Add the cubed aubergine, half of the sliced chilli, a tablespoon of tamarind and the muscovado sugar. Stir-fry for 5 minutes until the aubergine is golden and beginning to soften.

**Add** the cooked rice, mint, spinach and the remaining tamarind to the aubergine and onion mixture. Continue to stir-fry for 5–6 minutes or until piping hot.

**Sprinkle** over the remaining chilli slices. Season with salt and pepper and serve immediately.

**For tamarind & dill rice**, replace the aubergines with 2 finely diced courgettes and use 8 tablespoons finely chopped fresh dill, instead of the mint. Proceed as above, omitting the chilli slices.

# chilli, lemon & pea pulao

Serves **4**
Preparation time **10 minutes**,
  plus standing
Cooking time **about 15
  minutes**

1 tablespoon **light olive oil**
10 **curry leaves**
2 **dried Kashmiri red chillies**,
  broken into large pieces
2 **cassia bark sticks**
2–3 **cloves**
4–6 green **cardamom pods**,
  crushed
2 teaspoons **cumin seeds**
¼ teaspoon **ground turmeric**
250 g (8 oz) **basmati rice**,
  rinsed and drained
4 tablespoons **lemon juice**
500 ml (17 fl oz) hot
  **vegetable stock**
200 g (7 oz) fresh or frozen
  **peas**
**salt** and **pepper**

**Heat** the oil in a nonstick saucepan over a medium heat. Add the curry leaves, chilli, cassia bark, cloves, cardamom, cumin seeds and turmeric. Stir-fry for 20–30 seconds, then add the rice. Stir-fry for 2 minutes until the grains are well coated.

**Add** the lemon juice, stock and peas, season to taste and bring to the boil. Reduce the heat to low, cover the pan and cook gently for 10–12 minutes or until all the liquid has been absorbed. Remove from the heat and allow to stand, covered and undisturbed, for 10–15 minutes. Fluff up the grains with a fork and serve.

**For chilli, mixed bean & dill rice**, follow the recipe above, but replace the peas with a 400 g (13 oz) can mixed beans, rinsed and drained, and the chopped coriander with a large handful of finely chopped dill. Serve with fat-free natural yogurt.

# chickpea & spinach curry

Serves **4**

Preparation time **20 minutes**, plus soaking

Cooking time **about 1 hour**

200 g (7 oz) **dried chickpeas**

1 tablespoon **groundnut oil**

2 **onions**, thinly sliced

2 teaspoons **ground coriander**

2 teaspoons **ground cumin**

1 teaspoon **hot chilli powder**

½ teaspoon **ground turmeric**

1 tablespoon **medium curry powder** (see page 16)

400 g (13 oz) can **chopped tomatoes**

1 teaspoon **soft brown sugar**

100 ml (3½ fl oz) **water**

2 tablespoons chopped **mint leaves**

100 g (3½ oz) **baby spinach**

**salt**

**Place** the chickpeas in a deep bowl and cover with cold water. Leave to soak overnight. Transfer to a colander and rinse under cold running water. Drain and place in a wok. Cover with water and bring to the boil, then reduce the heat to low. Simmer gently for 45 minutes, skimming off any scum that rises to the surface and stirring often. Drain and set aside.

**Meanwhile,** heat the oil in the wok, add the onions and cook over a low heat for 15 minutes until lightly golden. Add the coriander, cumin, chilli powder, turmeric and curry powder and stir-fry for 1–2 minutes. Add the tomatoes, sugar and the measured water and bring to the boil. Cover, reduce the heat and simmer gently for 15 minutes.

**Add** the chickpeas, season to taste and cook gently for 8–10 minutes. Stir in the chopped mint. Divide the spinach leaves between 4 shallow bowls and top with the chickpea mixture. Serve immediately with steamed rice or bread.

**For curry-filled baked sweet potatoes**, scrub 4 small sweet potatoes under cold running water, then prick with a fork. Cook in a preheated oven at 200°C (400°F), Gas Mark 6, for about 1 hour, until tender. Split the sweet potatoes in half and fill with the curry, prepared as above. Top with yogurt and serve.

# rice with shiitake mushrooms

Serves **4**
Preparation time **10 minutes**,
  plus soaking and standing
Cooking time **about 25
  minutes**

300 g (10 oz) **basmati rice**,
  rinsed and drained
2 tablespoons **groundnut oil**
400 g (13 oz) **shiitake
  mushrooms**, sliced
1 **fresh red chilli**, deseeded
  and finely chopped
1 tablespoon **mild curry
  powder** (see page 16)
1 **cinnamon stick**
2 teaspoons **cumin seeds**
2 **cloves**
4 green **cardamom pods**,
  lightly bruised
8 **black peppercorns**
4 tablespoons **crisp-fried
  onions** (available from Asian
  grocers)
200 g (7 oz) fresh or frozen
  **peas**
700 ml (1 pint 3½ fl oz) hot
  **vegetable stock**

**Soak** the rice in a bowl of cold water for 20 minutes,
then drain thoroughly. Heat the oil in a large saucepan
over a high heat. Add the mushrooms and stir-fry for
6–8 minutes.

**Add** the chilli, curry powder, spices and crisp-fried
onions. Stir-fry for 2–3 minutes, then add the peas and
stir-fry for a further 2–3 minutes. Add the rice, and stir
for a minute or so to coat the grains.

**Add** the stock, season to taste and bring to the boil.
Reduce the heat to low, cover the pan and cook gently
for 10–12 minutes or until all the liquid has been
absorbed. Remove from the heat and allow to stand,
covered and undisturbed, for 10–15 minutes. Fluff up
the grains with a fork and serve with salad.

**For quick spicy mushroom fried rice**, heat
1 tablespoon groundnut oil in a nonstick frying pan.
Add 8 sliced spring onions, 1 sliced red chilli, 400 g
(13 oz) sliced shiitake mushrooms and 4 sliced garlic
cloves, and stir-fry for 5–6 minutes. Add 400 g (13 oz)
cold cooked long-grain rice, 1 teaspoon sesame oil
and 4 tablespoons light soy sauce. Stir-fry for 3–4
minutes or until piping hot and serve immediately.

# spicy lentil & basmati pilau

Serves **4**

Preparation time **15 minutes**, plus standing

Cooking time **20–25 minutes**

1 tablespoon **groundnut oil**

1 **onion**, finely chopped

1 teaspoon **ground turmeric**

1 tablespoon **cumin seeds**

1 **dried red chilli**

1 **cinnamon stick**

3 **cloves**

½ teaspoon **cardamom seeds**, crushed

225 g (7½ oz) **basmati rice**, rinsed

125 g (4 oz) **dried red lentils** (masoor dhal), rinsed

600 ml (1 pint) **vegetable stock**

6 tablespoons finely chopped **coriander leaves**

**salt**

**Heat** the oil in a large saucepan over a medium heat. Add the onion, stir-fry for 6–8 minutes until very soft, then add the spices. Continue to stir-fry for 2–3 minutes until fragrant. Now add the rice and lentils, and stir-fry for a further 2–3 minutes.

**Add** the stock and coriander, season to taste and bring to the boil. Reduce the heat to low, cover the pan and cook gently for 10–12 minutes or until all the liquid has been absorbed. Remove from the heat and allow to stand, covered and undisturbed, for 10–15 minutes. Fluff up the grains with a fork and serve.

**For tamarind, curry leaf & coconut relish**, to serve as an accompaniment, soak 2 teaspoons dried yellow split peas in cold water for 2–3 hours, drain and set aside. Place 200 g (7 oz) grated fresh coconut, 2 chopped green chillies and a large pinch of sea salt in a food processor and blend to a fine paste, adding a little water if necessary. Transfer to a bowl. Heat 1 tablespoon groundnut oil in a small frying pan and add 2 teaspoons mustard seeds and the lentils. Cover and cook over a gentle heat until you hear the mustard seeds starting to 'pop'. Add 6 curry leaves and 1 dried red chilli and stir-fry for 1 minute. Add the spices and 2 teaspoons tamarind paste to the coconut mixture and stir to mix well. Season to taste.

# thai spiced fried rice

Serves **4**
Preparation time **5 minutes**,
 plus soaking
Cooking time **about 15
 minutes**

225 g (7½ oz) **jasmine rice**
1 tablespoon **groundnut oil**
6 **spring onions**, finely
 chopped
4 teaspoons finely chopped
 **lemon grass** (tough outer
 leaves removed)
2 **fresh red chillies**, deseeded
 and finely chopped
1 tablespoon **Thai green curry
 paste** (see page 17)
500 ml (17 fl oz) **boiling water**
100 ml (3½ fl oz) **reduced-fat
 coconut milk**
**salt**
**Thai basil**, to garnish

**Wash** the rice in several changes of cold water, then drain. Soak in a bowl of fresh cold water for 15 minutes, then drain thoroughly.

**Heat** the oil in a large saucepan over a medium heat and add the spring onions, lemon grass, chillies, curry paste and drained rice. Stir-fry for 2–3 minutes until fragrant and the rice grains are evenly coated.

**Add** the measured boiling water and the coconut milk. Stir to mix well, season to taste and bring to the boil. Reduce the heat to low, cover the pan and cook gently for 10–12 minutes or until all the liquid has been absorbed. Remove from the heat and allow to stand, covered and undisturbed, for 10–15 minutes. Fluff up the grains with a fork and serve immediately, garnished with Thai basil.

**For Thai bean sprout & peanut salad**, to serve as an accompaniment, toss 150 g (5 oz) bean sprouts in a salad bowl with ½ thinly sliced cucumber, 3 shredded spring onions, 1 finely chopped red chilli, 1 carrot, cut into matchsticks, and a small handful each of mint and Thai basil leaves. Make a dressing by mixing 1 tablespoon Thai fish sauce with 1 tablespoon lime juice and 1 teaspoon agave syrup. When ready to serve, pour the dressing over the salad, toss to coat and scatter with 50 g (2 oz) chopped roasted peanuts.

# Thai rice with pork & beans

Serves **4**

Preparation time **15 minutes**

Cooking time **15–20 minutes**

1 tablespoon **groundnut oil**

2–3 tablespoons **Thai red curry paste** (see page 17)

375 g (12 oz) **lean pork fillet**, finely sliced

250 g (8 oz) **snake beans** or **French beans**, cut into 2.5 cm (1 inch) lengths

15 g (½ oz) **palm sugar** or **brown sugar**

750 g (1½ lb) cold cooked **jasmine rice**

1½ tablespoons **Thai fish sauce**

**salt**

3–4 **kaffir lime leaves,** finely shredded, to garnish

**Heat** the oil in a wok or large frying pan over a medium heat and stir-fry the curry paste for 3–4 minutes or until fragrant. Add the pork and stir-fry for 4–5 minutes.

**Add** the beans and sugar, stir-fry for another 4–5 minutes, then add the rice and fish sauce and stir-fry for 3–4 minutes more. Season to taste, divide between 4 warmed serving plates and garnish with shredded lime leaves.

**For rice with spicy vegetables**, heat 1 tablespoon groundnut oil in a large wok or frying pan over a medium heat and stir-fry 2–3 tablespoons Thai red curry paste for 3–4 minutes or until fragrant. Add 625 g (1¼ lb) mixed sugarsnap peas and baby sweetcorn and stir-fry for 3–4 minutes. Add 750 g (1½ lb) cold cooked jasmine rice and 2–2½ tablespoons light soy sauce and stir-fry for another 3–4 minutes or until the rice has just warmed through. Serve immediately.

# tomato & fennel rice

Serves **4**

Preparation time **20 minutes**,
  plus soaking and standing

Cooking time **about
  20 minutes**

275 g (9 oz) **basmati rice**

3 tablespoons **sunflower oil**

4 **shallots**, finely chopped

2 teaspoons **fennel seeds**

2 **garlic cloves**, finely chopped

4 ripe **tomatoes**, skinned,
  deseeded and finely
  chopped

500 ml (17 fl oz) **hot water**

2 tablespoons finely chopped
  fresh **coriander**

**salt** and **pepper**

**Wash** the rice several times in cold water, then leave to soak for 15 minutes. Drain thoroughly.

**Heat** the oil in a heavy-based saucepan and fry the shallots, fennel and garlic for 4—5 minutes. Add the tomatoes and rice and stir-fry for 2—3 minutes. Season well and pour over the measured hot water. Cover tightly, reduce the heat and simmer gently for 10 minutes. Do not lift the lid, as the steam is required for the cooking process.

**Remove** the pan from the heat and leave the rice to stand, covered and undisturbed, for 8—10 minutes. Fluff up the grains with a fork, stir in the fresh coriander and serve immediately.

**For cherry tomato & almond rice**, replace the fennel seeds with an equal quantity of coarsely crushed coriander seeds and use 250 g (8 oz) halved cherry tomatoes instead of diced tomatoes. When you fluff up the rice, add 2 tablespoons toasted flaked almonds.

# index

237

# acknowledgements

**Executive editor:** Eleanor Maxfield
**Editor:** Alex Stetter
**Executive art editor:** Juliette Norsworthy
**Designer:** Penny Stock
**Photographer:** Will Heap
**Home economist:** Denise Smart
**Props stylist:** Kim Sullivan
**Senior production controller:** Caroline Alberti

**Special photography:** © Octopus Publishing Group Limited/Will Heap
**Other photography:** Octopus Publishing Group/ Stephen Conroy 13, 15 top, 18, 81, 82, 91, 93, 99, 101, 109, 117, 139, 217, 223; /Neil Mersh 121; /David Munns 6, 44; /Lis Parsons 69, 145, 167, 201, 203, 207; /William Shaw 9, 51, 61, 113; /Eleanor Skan 16, 231; /Ian Wallace 12, 15 bottom, 105, 124, 154, 163, 189, 192. Thinkstock/iStockphoto 10, 11, 14.